The ENCOURAGED *Parent*

What Matters Publishing House

IVAN TAIT

Copyright © 2020 Ivan Tait
All rights reserved. Except as permitted under the U.S. Copyright
Act of 1976, no part of this publication may be reproduced,
distributed, or transmitted in any form or by any means, or stored in a database or
retrieval system, without the prior written permission of the publisher.

Scripture quotations marked AMP are from The Amplified Bible, Old Testament
copyright © 1965, 1987 by the Zondervan Corporation. The Amplified Bible, New
Testament copyright © 1954, 1958, 1987 by The Lockman Foundation. Used by
permission. All rights reserved.

Scripture quotations are taken from the Holy Bible, New Living Translation,
copyright ©1996, 2004, 2007, 2013, 2015 by Tyndale House Foundation. Used by
permission of Tyndale House Publishers, Inc., Carol Stream, Illinois 60188. All
rights reserved.

Scripture quotations are taken from The Holy Bible, English Standard Version®
(ESV®). Copyright ©2001 by Crossway Bibles, a division of Good News Publishers. Used by permission. All rights reserved.

Scripture quotations marked NIV are taken from the Holy Bible, New International
Version®. NIV®. Copyright © 1973, 1978, 1984 by International Bible Society.
Used by permission of Zondervan. All rights reserved.

Scripture quotations marked "NKJV™" are taken from the New King James Ver-
sion®. Copyright © 1982 by Thomas Nelson, Inc. Used by permission. All rights
reserved.

Published by
What Matters Ministries and Missions Publishing
ISBN   978-0-9893060-6-5

Design and Layout: What Matters Ministries and Missions
Printed in USA

INTRODUCTION

To love a child is divinity; to be loved by a child is Heaven! As parents, we hurt when our children hurt. We hurt twice as much when our children make choices that create hurt and pain for themselves. We long to give them the wisdom and lessons of our lives. We wish we could spare them all the pain we have felt. To see them choose wisely is one of life's greatest blessings.

Here in this book, I have endeavored to give you the parent's divine tools of personal encouragement. I have designed this book as a source of daily and continual blessing. A parent that is faith-filled is fear-free. Encouragement is the gasoline in our parental tanks. Encouragement gives us patience, strength, faith, and joy. In parenting, your children are your treasure; they hold your heart in their hands. Since the day they were born, you have been connected to them biologically, emotionally, spiritually, and in all those inexplicable ways which only a parent can know. Here in this book, you will find letters from God for you, divine encouragement that will give you the daily bread you need to do the most and be the most for your children. In our times, there is a holocaust of lost children. Everywhere we look, we see the signs of children with no compass. We watch as they are snatched from their God-built cocoons and seduced by the strategies of darkness. Never has it been so important to be a wise, connected, consistent, enlightened parent. Never has it been this necessary to hold in your hands the divine keys that will unlock the storehouses of Heaven for your children. Never before have we, as parents, needed so much encouragement from God. Encouragement is a parent's armor from God against the missiles of evil.

I have also included prophetic prayers with a prophetic anointing that will elevate your children and set them on the path to their destiny. By praying the word of God prophetically, you activate the divine powers of Heaven and release the Holy Spirit's boundless assistance. Prophetic prayers change the plans of darkness. You will see the visible divinities rise in your children. You will be able to grasp the power of the impossibilities of activated faith. By reading these letters from God, you will glean the nuggets of divine sight, gather the blessings of divine wisdom, and see into your child's spiritual climate. As you pray these prophetic prayers, your family will dwell in the hollow of God's hand, and you will stand as a guard over the potential of your children. Remember, an encouraged parent is a sword no devil can thwart!

To all parents who believe in and battle for your children's destiny, I dedicate this book to equip and empower your destiny as their parent.

THE FEAR OF THE LORD

Fear of the LORD is the foundation of true knowledge, but fools despise wisdom and discipline. Proverbs 1:7 (NLT)

The Fear of the Lord is a destiny conviction. Without it, no destiny can be fulfilled. Those who fear me have no other masters, no other ruling fears. They bow to no one. They cannot be threatened or bribed, bullied or seduced. Those that fear me, please me. They sleep in peace, untroubled by anyone's ravings. The darkness cannot alarm them, they cannot be bought and will not sell out. They overflow with death-defying courage. Because they fear me, they persuade men and women to love me. Good fear, the fear of the Lord, is the end of all inner conflict. What you fear rules you. Godly fear breeds deep respect. The fear of the Lord is your children's protection, it will keep them in the hollow of my hand. It will release them from the slings and arrows of Satan's lies. Your children shall be comforted, enjoying untroubled peace. They will esteem my name. I have taken away my judgment and they will not fear disaster for I will clear away their enemies. I will revive whatever they pray over, for it is sound wisdom to fear me. I will destroy the idols of the heart from my house and cleanse the altars and sanctuaries. I will open the rain window and pour out showers of favor. I will come in like a rushing stream. I will be the stability of their times and reveal to them the location of the storehouses of wealth. Riches, honor and life shall pursue them all the days of their lives. I will open the fountain of life and they shall drink from it all of their lives.

TODAY I PRAY...

Psalm 84:11 over my child. No good thing will be withheld from them. The Lord will be their Sun and their Shield and they will be full of glory all day long and no one will steal the precious ideas of the Holy Spirit from them.

...IN THE NAME OF JESUS.

THE SOUND OF DELIVERANCE

It was for this freedom that Christ set us free [completely liberating us]; therefore keep standing firm and do not be subject again to a yoke of slavery [which you once removed]. Galatians 5:1 (AMP)

Your children shall hear the sound of deliverance. Victory shouts shall overtake them. Through every snare and trial, every lie and deception, every trap, assassin and temptation, deliverance will arise for them, for I will preserve them in trouble. I will bring them out of every pit of compromise. I will lead them by my eye and grant them counsel and strength. I will keep them alive and safe from vile venom and snakes. My hand shall be at work in their lives and on their behalf. Blessings shall come to them. They shall attack the 12 giants of life and win. They shall sever the heads of the tyrant masters and ring the bells of liberty. Great strength shall be theirs. Great victories shall come for them and through them. I will be their watchtower, their viewpoint, their perspective, their perception, their conclusion. I am their hiding place. I will cocoon them in safety and surround them with peace and quietness. Those that are pregnant with death shall be delivered from the demon seeds. Those that mourn in silence shall be unplugged and defused. Those that writhe in pain shall find relief and comfort. There is a sound coming, the sound of deliverance in the land. I have anointed them to announce freedom to the captives, freedom from the corruption and from their personal inner weaknesses. They shall be the ambassadors of deliverance to their world.

TODAY I PRAY...

2 Corinthians 9:8 over my child, that God will make all grace abound toward them, that they will have all sufficiency in all things and will abound to every good work

...IN THE NAME OF JESUS.

THE YOKE BREAKER

"And in that day his burden will depart from your shoulder, and his yoke from your neck; and the yoke will be broken because of the fat." Isaiah 10:27 (ESV)

Your children began as little breaths of divinity but will end up as cyclones of transformation. They are bulldozers, demolition experts in the powers of yoke and bondage destruction. They seem unintimidating, but when I am finished with them the enemy shall tremble at their power, might and force. The sword shall be alive and active, able to detect bondage and destroy it. They shall set at peace those restless with anxiety. They shall seize the spoil from the slavers. They shall break the yoke of sin off the neck of the oppressed. They shall lead multitudes out of the bondage of Egypt, destroying the old taskmasters with their tormenting whips. They shall dry up the old mud pits of addiction and inner tyranny. They shall break the bars of iron and make the bent over to stand upright and run. They are the yokeless deliverers. The emancipation of mental jails, emotional prisons and the torture chambers of fear is theirs. They shall end poverty, hunger, thirst and soul nakedness. They shall melt the iron yokes into ashes. They have the yoke breaking anointing; the rod of offenses shall be dissolved. Not even the memory of the bondage shall survive. The hand, feet, shoulders and neck shall be freed. The shackles shall burst and explode. Wherever they walk, you will disintegrate the yokes of Babylon and the bondage of Egypt shall cease to exist. The people shall have deliverers and liberators. They shall feel the full powers of my Son's victories at Calvary! Life, Liberty, and Love shall become the new yokes of their lives!

TODAY I PRAY...

2 Corinthians 12:9 over my children, that God's grace is sufficient for them today. His strength is made perfect in their weakness. They will abound and overflow with good deeds today and be filled with the holiness of God.

...IN THE NAME OF JESUS.

WINGS THAT CANNOT BE BROKEN

He gives power to the faint, and to him who has no might he increases strength.
Even youths shall faint and be weary, and young men shall fall exhausted; but they
who wait for the Lord shall renew their strength; they shall mount up with
wings like eagles; they shall run and not be weary; they shall walk and not faint.
Isaiah 40:29-31 (ESV)

I have given your children wings that cannot be broken. Their spiritual flight will not be stopped or delayed by brokenness or wounds. Their life of flight will take them to paradises of redemption. Unbroken wings create achievements of faith. I will make them competent and equipped for every good work. They are artists of achievement. They shall wave high the banner of divine success, for through my Son they can do all things unreasonably well. They shall sound the trumpet of success, for the armies of success, for those born to fly, to cover great lengths of earth and sky. They shall feed the poor, rescue the orphans, build great rescue houses and turn the useless into masterpieces of achievement. The mentors of flight shall arise from your children. Their rewards shall be obvious to all. Be of good cheer, for I have imprisoned the wing clippers. I have caged them, chained them and locked them up, for your children shall be children of substance. Faith is the evidence of their credibility. They shall take their stand at the watchtower of purpose and call out in the day and night. When they come to the waters and drink, they shall abolish dead man's philosophies, traditions, empty conceits and vanity, and fly. Those who sincerely seek My mind find the place where no crippling fear lives, the place perfect love originates. To love perfectly is to fly unhindered, without broken wings, in an unlimited faith-flight, with the powers of the currents of the wind soaring under Me.

TODAY I PRAY...

Acts 1:8 over my children. They will be filled with the Holy Spirit and baptized in the fire of the Holy Ghost and will consume all the sin around them by the flaming fire of God that proceeds out of them.

...IN THE NAME OF JESUS.

WHAT HONORS IS DIVINE

Pray for us, for we are sure that we have a clear conscience, desiring to act honorably in all things. Hebrews 13:18 (ESV)

Honor is the ability to see both the invisible and the visible value in others. A child who feels honored, honors. A child who observes honor, becomes honorable. Honor is a cleansing power. It preserves the value of those who are unvalued. Whatever you honor converts you. I will place honor in and around your children. They shall carry honor like a vaccine, a medicine of the soul. Anything that is honored rises. Honor creates the skeleton of a life of love. Honor is the framework for all divine favor. I will give honor to your children. I will promote them and cause them to respect all mankind. Their honoring will heal the disrespect of the world. They shall add divine qualities to the uncherished, those only seen by Me. They shall plant the seeds of pricelessness in the forsaken. They shall sow immortality, eternity and divinity into the unvalued generations of life. Those who honor Me, I will honor-with undefiled, unbutchered, unbroken, unviolated life; life which is free from viruses, germs, and bacteria of the mind and diseases of thought. Your children shall have the gifts of honor: blessed homes, families and deeds. Honor washes the soul with soap. It purifies the motives of self-promotion. It redefines the identity and changes the impulses of the DNA. It creates an atmosphere of genuineness. It abhors evil and holds fast to what is good. Your children shall reshape the world with honor's gifts. Honor is divine, making the worthless priceless.

TODAY I PRAY...

Psalm 63:1-3 over my children. They will be desperate for God all day long, loving him, longing for Him, and obeying Him. They will see God in His whole power as they pray and worship in His presence.

...IN THE NAME OF JESUS.

THE GRACE MOLD

And God is able to make all grace abound to you, so that having all sufficiency in all things at all times, you may abound in every good work. 2 Corinthians 9:8 (ESV)

I will place your children in My grace mold. The place of divinity's hands, sculpted, molded and designed by grace. A place of entering sufficiency; A place of unmerited achievements, accomplishments and awe-inspiring exploits. My grace will lead them. I will impart to them the ability to trust my grace in them. They shall renounce their weakness, drink my power and become super-efficient achievers of grace works. All deeds are worthless unless achieved by motives of grace and love's intentions. My grace will be made perfect in their insufficiencies, for they shall stand inside my saving grace and guide the masses to it. Their personality shall be grace covered. Sin shall have no dominion over them, for they shall become invisible ambassadors of goodness through my grace. They shall work tirelessly day and night, accomplishing unnatural works of beauty. They shall produce unmistakable works of divinity. They shall have unlimited confidence and live at My throne of grace. They shall receive daily mercies and yearly breakthroughs. They shall be filled to overflowing with My fullness, going from grace to grace while living in the grace mold. They will be trained by My Spirit to renounce and dispel ungodliness, worldly passions and to live self-controlled, upright, godly lives. Mocking the devil with success, they shall stomp out loneliness from the weak-willed and double-minded. My word will become tangible, Christ-likeness in action, revealing the rich mercy and kindness of my love. The grace mold is the safe life; grace saves the unsaveable and transforms the unthinkable.

TODAY I PRAY...

Psalm 27:1-2 over my children. The Lord will be their Light today and their Salvation. They will not be afraid of anything or anyone. They will not be intimidated by peer pressure, friends, or bullies.

...IN THE NAME OF JESUS.

GIFT WRAPPED

The name of the Lord is a strong tower; the righteous man runs into it and is safe.
Proverbs 18:10 (ESV)

A man's gift makes room for him and places him or her before great men. I am gift-wrapping your children with divine abilities and talents. I will touch their hearts and put holy desires in them to learn skills and special abilities. They shall perform acts of wonder. Their gifts shall become platforms of inspiration for the ungifted. They shall learn the skills of devotion, practice and disciplined learning. They shall live gift-wrapped. They shall use their gifts to heal and inspire the young and old; for every good gift comes from above. From Me, the Father of lights, the Father of clarity, the Father of the undeserved insights comes every good gift. The gift-wrapped child is an unopened gift of potential; a sleeping, unopened gift of divine surprises and encounters. The gifts I give are irrevocable. The gifts shall make your children highly favored in their lives. They shall walk among kings and rulers of the world. They shall reveal their gifts and transform a kingdom. I will fill your children with My Holy Spirit. I place my wisdom in their minds. They shall see what is broken and sick. They are gift-wrapped by me. I will give them divine intelligence, knowledge, craftsmanship and artistic design in all manner of workmanship. They shall be geniuses of design, experts of creative ideas, teachers and mentors of the divine touch.

TODAY I PRAY...

2 Timothy 1:7 over my children. They will know God has not given them the spirit of fear or timidity, but instead they have a sound mind that thinks clearly and perfectly. They have the spirit of power that removes the enemy from their path and they are filled with the Spirit of Love for those that treat them well and those that treat them poorly.

...IN THE NAME OF JESUS.

HELD BY WONDER

For you created my inmost being; you knit me together in my mother's womb.
Psalm 139:13 (NIV)

Worship is wonder in control. Worship is being wrapped in My nature. Worship is obeying when you don't want to. They shall be held by wonder. Their eyes shall see the King in His beauty. They shall be transfixed by the beauties of My Son's perfect love; captured by the unreasonableness of grace and the unearned benefits of faith in action. They shall be prisoners of wonder, held forever in the grip of My unspeakable goodness. They shall be eternally captured by My revealed and divine beauty. They shall know wonder, awe, speechlessness, amazement and the completeness of being possessed by divine beauty. They shall never wander from the path of life or turn to the right or left. They shall be like flint, aiming at eternity, fixed on the target of eternal purpose. They shall approach the unapproachable Light and be transfigured by it. They shall see Him Who is altogether lovely, in Whom there is no flaw. They shall glow with the glory of encounter. Their inner being shall be held in the wonder of discovery and chasing. The hidden manna shall be theirs. The imperishable beauty shall be the reward of their unflinching obedience. Your children are trophies of wonder. They are fearfully and wonderfully made. I have placed eternity in their hearts. I have stamped my image in their minds and painted the invisible parts of me on the canvas of their spirit. They shall be held firmly in the grace of wonder year after year. I am a wonder to behold and they, a wonder to be.

TODAY I PRAY...

Psalm 34:4 over my children. When they cry to the Lord, He delivers them from their intimidations and peer pressure and situations. They are in perfect peace at school and around any dominant personalities.

...IN THE NAME OF JESUS.

THE BUILDER'S MIND

You yourselves like living stones are being built up as a spiritual house, to be a holy priesthood, to offer spiritual sacrifices acceptable to God through Jesus Christ.
1 Peter 2:5 (ESV)

You are not a collector of worthless driftwood. You are building kingdom generals, leaders, and commanders of the armies of heaven. The training for a general or a builder is not the same as the training of a private or a potato peeler. You are a parent endowed with great and gifted children. I will teach you the secrets of divine isolation. In sacred isolation, you become invisible and I become visible. To teach this secret to your children is to guarantee them success in life. No one reigns without a master of truth. No one conquers without divine intelligence. No one conquers life without sacred surrender. In selling everything, you are given everything. Your children have been chosen to dread nothing, to be beyond intimidation. The builder's mind will be my gift to your children, the ability to see things and people built and complete. The gift of completing a project, resting after completion and starting anew again. The great builders of the world, create, invent, and visualize pieces of heaven and bring them into reality. When love comes to their door, he will teach them how to take the throw-aways and turn them into masterpieces of love. What's built with love is indestructible. I am the materials: the cement, wood and steel. I am the foundation, the walls and kitchens. I am the floor and ceiling, the paint and plumbing. Everything they will need, I will provide, divinely built. Their life will be remembered, celebrated and eternally admired by thousands for leaving an eternal legacy of hope.

TODAY I PRAY...

Psalm 37:4 over my children. The Lord will give them the desires of their heart. They will learn as they walk in fellowship with God, that He wants to give them the keys to His kingdom. They will know, beyond a shadow of a doubt, that their life will be rich and full of the Holy Spirit's blessings.

...IN THE NAME OF JESUS.

A DIET OF DIVINITY

Oh, taste and see that the Lord is good! Blessed is the man who takes refuge in him!
Psalm 34:8 (ESV)

What you feed grows, what you starve dies. The diet of divinity is the only true nourishment your children can thrive on. They will never survive on the food of the flesh or the desserts of the soul. Their food must be cooked by Calvary, seasoned with faith and marinated in love. The diet of divinity is that which I have created to nourish me in them. The divine diet consists of all the mysteries of faith. They will grow in their faith skills and develop mountain-moving powers. They shall be known as water walkers. They shall raise those dead in indifference from their lethal. They shall walk by faith and not by sight. They shall cause movement towards me. They shall heal the sick and let the prisoners go free. They shall be doubtless in conviction, bold as lions and guiltless, shameless proclaimers of my gospel. Your children shall be fed the delicacies of true unbiased love. They shall master selflessness and be humble foot washers. All people shall be sacred to them. They shall be famous for loving the rejected, downtrodden people of the world. The diet of divinity shall save them from the poisoned wormwood of Satan's table. The diet I give them will breed their superpowers. They shall fly where others crawl and soar where others drown. Children of divine hunger always hunger for more and are never satisfied with what displeases the divine. They shall have perfect inner peace and a raging passion for more of me.

TODAY I PRAY...

Isaiah 40:29-31 over my children. They will mount up with wings like an eagle. They will soar at school. They will glide over trouble and temptation. They will exchange their weaknesses for God's strengths. They will run and not grow weary. They will walk and not faint in any difficult situation.

...IN THE NAME OF JESUS.

CHASING THE PRIZE

Brothers, I do not consider that I have made it my own. But one thing I do: forgetting what lies behind and straining forward to what lies ahead, I press on toward the goal for the prize of the upward call of God in Christ Jesus. Philippians 3:13-14 (ESV)

There is a prize so valuable that men and women throughout the ages have been willing to die for it. They have jumped into the fire, been pierced with the sword, sawed asunder, and extinguished by the power of the sword. Through their escape of the raging fires and out of their frailty and weakness, they won strength. They became mighty and stalwart over their resisters in battle. Others were tortured to death with clubs, refusing relief in order to gain the prize. Rejecting the powers that be, others suffered mocking, jumped into the lion's mouth, drank pain, and endured scourging and chains. Imprisonment came as a reward; yet others were stoned to death, tempted, bribed, intimidated and bullied without compromise. Still others were slaughtered while alive, wrapped in the skins of sheep and goats, left utterly destitute, oppressed, and cruelly treated. These men and women, of whom the world was not worthy, did it all for the prize. These will be your children: unflinching in battle, unmoved by temptation, unhindered by torture, unstoppable, invincible champions of faith, winners of the crown and prize.

TODAY I PRAY...

Genesis 2:7 over my children. God, their Heavenly Father, will breathe into their nostrils the living breath of Heaven. They will not speak like normal children, but they will speak like Jesus' children filled with wisdom, insight, perception, and divine perspectives about life.

...IN THE NAME OF JESUS.

THE POWER OF CONNECTION

Behold, I have given you authority to tread on serpents and scorpions, and over all the power of the enemy, and nothing shall hurt you. Luke 10:19 (ESV)

I will baptize your children in wonder working power. Their life will be a movement, a divine intervention. No enemy will feel comfortable in their presence, for I will give them the spirit of might, love and power. I will give them a divine mind. They shall become my trumpets throughout the world. They shall dance on the enemy's head. I will give them authority over serpents, scorpions and over all the strategies of the enemy. Nothing shall hurt, wound or cripple them. I will immerse them in strength. They shall give power to the faint and might to the tired and weary. The exhausted shall be refreshed. They shall mount up with wings like eagles and reach unreachable heights of power. They shall have unnatural powers of patience and endurance to last, and last, and last. Longevity will be their coat of armor; inexhaustible energy will push them forward. I will anoint them with a yoke breaking anointing and purpose them to destroy burdens and break chains. They will walk the earth releasing the oppressed and doing acts of goodness. All their days shall be marked by miracles. I will grant to them all things that pertain to life and godliness. They shall be masters of the living active word. They shall separate the chaff from the wheat, the fool's gold from the genuine gold. They shall know the immeasurable greatness of my power. The eyes of their heart will stay open and understand the hope of their calling and what their inheritance is. They shall be shameless proclaimers of the powers of the cross and part the Red Sea for thousands to cross safely.

TODAY I PRAY...

Song of Solomon 4:16 over my children. They are the garden of the Lord and He is making sure the soil of their heart remains soft, tender, and free from stumps, rocks, worms, thorns, and thistles.

...IN THE NAME OF JESUS.

THE COURAGEOUS HEART

Be strong and courageous. Do not fear or be in dread of them, for it is the Lord your God who goes with you. He will not leave you or forsake you." Deuteronomy 31:6 (ESV)

There is a heart that knows no defeat. It runs from no one and nothing. It is steadfast in the face of fear and confident in the presence of overwhelming odds. It laughs at death. Standing in front of jeering crowds, it never bends the knee. It is tall in the face of ridicule. It is unashamed of the gospel of life. IT can withstand the most honorable pain and not cringe in the presence of torture. The unintimidated heart is the atmosphere of heaven. No tyrant can conquer it, no brute can make it yield. No army can make it fear. The courageous heart attacks when others would retreat, it loves when it should hate, forgives when it should take revenge. This courageous heart serves without resentment. It is kind when it should be cruel.
It shows mercy when faced with temptation. It ignores the siren voices. When threatened, it smiles and moves forward. The courageous heart will live inside your children. They shall be leaders of the brave, mentors of the elite armies of heaven. When darkness raises its head, the radiance of my Son's face will lighten the hearts of your family. Courage, bravery and furious boldness will lead the way to the courageous heart. Even death will seem as a grasshopper!

TODAY I PRAY...

Acts 2:1-6 over my children. As they wait on God and pray in their secret closet, the Spirit of the Lord will come upon them like a mighty, rushing wind. They will be filled with the Holy Spirit and their hearts will be filled with the powers of the Holy Spirit. They will speak the wisdom of God, the power of God, and the love of God.

...IN THE NAME OF JESUS.

THE PLACE OF SWEETENING

Be kind to one another, tenderhearted, forgiving one another, as God in Christ forgave you. Ephesians 4:32 (ESV)

Sweetness comes from having been changed by forgiveness. A sweet spirit is the crown of undeserved mercy. The sour-hearted spoil everyone they touch. They turn the ripe fruit into worm-infested rottenness. Sweetness is life, void of poison. The place of sweetening is a sacred place. Those that find it are never the same. A sweet spirit heals the bitter pools of life. Bitterness is what happens when you marinate in a pool of unforgiveness. The bitter die slow deaths of sourness. All beauty is devoured by the bitter taste. Ashes from perfect fruit, scorpions from true love, death from innocent life. The sweet place is the destination of your children. The place of sweetness is beautiful, and awe-inspiring. The child with a sweet spirit cannot be spoiled by rejection or defeated by disfavor. Those with a sweet spirit attract my presence. A tender heart is my home. The souls that live in tenderness cannot be bought, sold or bribed. They have found their home. Your children shall dwell in peaceable dwelling places because of their kindness. All healing comes from a tender heart. The child that heals, has seen me.

TODAY I PRAY...

Over my children John 14:21-23. As my children practice obedience and learn to obey the promptings and urges of the Holy Spirit, the Father and the Son will reveal themselves to them. They will know Jesus intimately and perfectly all the days of their life.

...IN THE NAME OF JESUS.

THE CALL OF THE ETERNAL

He has made everything beautiful in its time. Also He has put eternity in their hearts,
except that no one can find out the work that God does from beginning to end.
Ecclesiastes 3:11 (NKJV)

The eternal truths are the only true realities that matter. The eternal can change the temporal and turn the worthless into the priceless. When the eternal realities enter someone's life, that life is permanently changed. The eternal cannot be destroyed, burned, buried or decay. In the eternal is the only place where complete wholeness can be found. There is no corruption in the eternal. Eternal works are the only things you will bring with you at death. The eternal are the ingredients of heaven sown into the hearts of the chosen. The eternal places are the places where nothing dies, withers or burns to ashes. The eternal child thinks with my mind. Their minds will be untouched by man. Their way of concluding is divine. Their imagination is unlimited in its ability to believe that I can do anything. The eternal child is not of this earth. They have transcended the laws of the earth. They now have access to heavens resources. The eternal child will never live at the feet of emptiness. They will never waste their time and energies pursuing worthlessness. They live for the sacred and eat eternity. I can grant their sacred wants and make their sacred dreams come true. Your children will touch the hem of heaven and reach the golden throne. Eternity will drive their existence. The sound of eternity will become the sweetest sound to them.

TODAY I PRAY...

Psalm 73:24-27 over my children. They will know that they have the God of heaven as their Helper. Their hearts and their strength will not fail them. They will know beyond all doubt that the Lord is their strength and the strength of their heart. The nearness of God is their blessing and their goodness.

...IN THE NAME OF JESUS.

THE LIGHT BEARER

In the same way, let your light shine before others, so that they may see your good works and give glory to your Father who is in heaven. Matt. 5:16 (ESV)

Light removes doubt. It shatters fear, overcomes deadly expectations, makes faith stand up and empowers confidence. Light is the healer of death. Light expels the gossip of the inner voices of the soul. The light bearer is a moving hospital and a living, speaking cure. The light bearer brings revolution to the truth, where there is no shadow worship, no obscurity, no half-truth living. The light bearer is the guide of heaven's mysteries. Light expands itself everywhere it exists. Light kills the diseases of darkness. All evil is allergic to light; light and darkness are eternally divorced. There can be no marriage of light and darkness, no fellowship of ideas, no unity in purpose. Light repels all ideas born in darkness. Your children are light in the making. Every truth they learn makes the light brighter. Every lesson of truth makes them teachers of light. To drink light is to fill yourself with the capacities of divinity. To eat light is to fill your spirit with healing virtues. All light comes from me. I am the light of the world. I have ordained your children to be light bearers, torches of truth. What is revealed cannot be concealed, the open cannot be misinterpreted, the seen cannot be blinded. The light in your children is their salvation. Exposure to light silences the voice of Satan. Feed your children light and they will become addicts of life. Light is the place where defects go to die.

TODAY I PRAY...

Proverbs 10:24 over my children. The blessings of the Lord make them rich and He adds no sorrow to them, no grief, and no regrets. They will love Jesus without hesitation. His will is only ever for their good, and they will find it.

...IN THE NAME OF JESUS.

THE TASTE OF HEAVEN'S SPICES

Awake, O north wind, and come, O south wind! Blow upon my garden, let its spices flow. (She) Let my beloved come to his garden, and eat its choicest fruits. Song of Solomon 4:16 (ESV)

Every divine spice cures something. I am spice, I am variety in holiness. I am the seasoning and the diversity of holiness. I am the plague stopper. I give the sacred spices to the dead, dull and boring. I take the worthless of this world and make them priceless. I take the trash and make it treasure. I take the useless and make it divine. I spice up life with the fragrances of heaven. Spice creates appetites. My spices create a hunger for me and mine. Spices fill the air with expectancy and activate the divine language of the soul. My spices change the dreams of the useless. My spices heal the corpses of the soul. My spices ignite joy and release peace. Whenever the wind of my spirit blows, it brings the spices into your garden. This means your children will be spice spreaders. They will gather from the four winds the sacred healing spices that make the healing oils of the apothecaries. They shall raise the apothecaries from their graves. The spice gatherers are life spreaders. They change the atmosphere of my church. They usher in healing gifts. They release the miracle working powers of life. Your children will live for the taste of heaven's spice. They shall swim in beauty. They shall be evangelists of the glories of heaven. Spices change reality. Your children have already been issued the keys to the spice warehouses where boredom dies, distraction loses its power and idleness is cursed into dirt. The spice gatherers cannot be bribed with the taste of plastic pleasures and plastic fruit. Yours are children of the spice!

TODAY I PRAY...

Exodus 25:22-23 over my children. They will stand before the Ark of God's Presence and they will see the wings of the cherubim stretched out over them. Today they will have sweet communion and fellowship with their Heavenly Father and be at peace in their minds.

...IN THE NAME OF JESUS.

THE STAIRWAY TO HEAVEN

Your word is a lamp to my feet and a light to my path. Psalm 119:105 (ESV)

There is a stairway to heaven, a place of ascending and descending. Each child must find this stairway and master its steps. Some lead up and others lead down. The child who finds the stairway is guaranteed promotion, success and prosperity. I will touch your children and put in them my spirit of hunger. They will long for my stairway. They will dream about it and chase it all their lives. The stairway is a stairway of wisdom. The child who walks on this stairway throbs with truth. They never drink fatigue. Their legs do not grow weary. The hands are never limp. They follow, taste and chew on my word. They swallow and digest it with relish and delight. The stairway is their utopia, the place they find me. They walk, run, kneel and sing their way to me. A child who finds the stairway is not double-minded, short-sighted or burdened with sin. They know the hallowed places and understand the sacred places of divine deaths. They run and shout their way to me. They understand the true greatness of my kingdom. They live with unsealed lips. They sprout power and germinate faith. They wreak havoc on my enemies. Your children will not follow another. They are mine, I am theirs. The stairway leads to me and I am waiting.

TODAY I PRAY...

Matthew 4:19 over my children that they do not waste their time or procrastinate or follow empty pursuits. They are soul-winners, fishers of men and women. They capture the minds and hearts of men and women and other children at their school and in all endeavors of life.

...IN THE NAME OF JESUS.

SACRED DEPENDENCY

"I can do nothing on my own. As I hear, I judge, and my judgment is just, because I seek not my own will but the will of him who sent me..." John 5:30 (ESV)

To depend on me is to access me. To rely on me is to release me. To yield to me is to move out of the way. Total dependence on me brings total provision from me. A life of dependence is a life without worthless dust, without the agony of pain and deformities of rejection. The sting of life is silenced; the arrows of abuse are broken. Life lived in dependency is true freedom. Dependence releases the energy of grace. It recharges the batteries of life. Sacred dependence removes idols of the heart and mind. Dependence is the union of the human with the divine. Your children will learn to rely on, depend on and be absorbed by me. Total dependent children find their purpose, individuality, voice, platform, and their freedom from everyone and everything. The totally dependent become conduits of my power. My Son said "I can do nothing on my own." (John 5:30) In dependency, the cravings stop, temptations are overcome and idleness is replaced with purpose. The ugly soul dies, the beasts of Adam's seed die. Consistency take the driver's seat. The plow begins to work. Your children will be grafted into my nature. We will be one; one spirit, one mind, one heart, one goal. All of me for all of them. Nothing missing, all divine!

TODAY I PRAY...

Jeremiah 20:9 over my children. The Word of God will be inside of them like fire burning in their bones and they will be consumed with a desire to know the Word of God, to preach the Word of God, and to live the Word of God.

...IN THE NAME OF JESUS.

THE WARRIOR'S CHILD

"For though we walk in the flesh, we are not waging war according to the flesh. For the weapons of our warfare are not of the flesh but have divine power to destroy strongholds. 2 Corinthians 10:3-4 (ESV)

The warrior's life is a life of focused victory. The warrior is a child that has been trained in all the fighting arts. They can disarm any foe, out maneuver any enemy and out-strategize any attacker. The warrior sees life as an arena where battles must be fought and decided. They are not familiar with the spirit of cowardice. Their life is spent gladly for my cause. The warrior child is tough-minded, full of confidence in my ability to give them abilities. They rest on the victory side of faith. They dream of plundering, vanquishing and overtaking the enemy's land. They are fully engaged, fully sold out and fully committed. There is no retreat in them. No surrender, no capitulation. They fight until they win or die. Your children have been issued their training orders. They are preparing to do great exploits; which have never been seen before: rescue missions for captured souls, relief missions for the overwhelmed. Destroy the enemy at any cost, this is their code. Your children will destroy the strongholds of unbelief and capture the hidden predators. They will blow up the fortresses of ideologies that twist the minds of the young and cripple the faith of the weak. They will capture the storehouses of the thieves and the robbers of the sacred beliefs of life. They will restore the fortresses of the plundered. They will bring back the treasures of light that were stolen and hidden for generations. They will spend their lives distributing the wealth of my kingdom. The warrior child is the hero of heaven.

TODAY I PRAY...

Hebrews 4:12 over my children. They will know that the Word of the Lord is quick, able to perform instantaneous miracles when they speak and pray it. The Word of God is powerful, more powerful than any other weapon in the world. It is sharper than a two-edged sword, and will pierce and divide within their hearts, the soulish things of life and spiritual things of life.

...IN THE NAME OF JESUS.

THE ARMORED CHILD

Put on the whole armor of God, that you may be able to stand against the schemes of the devil. Ephesians 6:11 (ESV)

The armored child has been given the immunities of the Spirit. They have the power to repel assaults. The unarmored fall and crash under the onslaught of the arrows and spears of the enemy, while the armored child is outfitted with supernatural defenses and powerful offensive weapons. The armor worn by an armored child is divinely made with pieces of me, what I am and who I am. They are as invaluable, undefeatable, safe, protected and impenetrable as I am. What I am, they wear. Their mind is armored with faith philosophies. Their heart is covered in the tenderness of love. Their soul is covered in purity and their spirit is dressed in my virtues, total protection, and total coverage. At all times, the armored child knows the secrets of living by faith. They are skilled in disarming lies and breaking the strongholds of fear. Your children will never be food for the cannibals of this life. They will walk among the vicious and heartless and not be harmed. They will see pain and heal it. They will see the arrows and never be pierced beyond repair. Dread and trouble will not consume them; it will only come as breezes, ripples and riffs that they can manage. They are extraordinary, immovable trophies of my grace and love. Sleep safe, be at peace, smile at the future. Your children will repel with ease the worst that the enemy brings against them. The guarded instinctively guard the shielded cover. The nurtured, nurture and the unbroken, repair.

TODAY I PRAY...

Isaiah 55:10-11 over my children. They will receive the Word of the Lord like rain, like water, like snow. Their hearts are the fields in which God sews His Word and that Word which they are believing for today will not return to them void but will accomplish the thing that God sent it out to do.

...IN THE NAME OF JESUS.

THE OVERMASTERING DESIRES

Delight yourself in the Lord, and he will give you the desires of your heart.
Psalm 37:4 (ESV)

To manage the overmastering desires of life is the essence of greatness. The self-controlled have learned the secrets of trust. Uncontrolled desires open doors of disaster. A child who controls what he feels becomes a grant of virtue. Children born with flawed DNA require divine encounters to heal their natural tendencies. Your children will never see the self-built, self-inflicted prisons of the soul. Nor will they see altered realties or twisted expectations. Your child will shout from the rooftops the victories of Calvary. They will be my witnesses and my ambassadors of light to those who are chased by nagging desires. They will not underestimate latent wants, secret urges, or blistering impulses. For I will lead your children to the place of transfer, where their wants become my wants and their urges become my urges. My presence will become for them a cauldron of purification. Love will takeover the throne of desires within them. Love is selfishness imprisoned. I will teach them to master their meditations, for from these, they will grow strong and holy. The ruling part will be their inner life consecrated by love, perfected and united to me. The child raised in purity's arms has erased betrayals and discovered self-will. Your children will want what I want and live to serve it. They will have unsoiled spirits and unsullied souls. They will be fully mine and fully trusted.

TODAY I PRAY...

Isaiah 54:17 over my children. No weapon the enemy may form to hurt, deceive, or trap my children will prosper over them. No word that comes out of the mouth of any bully or unkind person will prevail over their spirit by discouraging or wounding them. They will have the armor of faith all around them today.

...IN THE NAME OF JESUS.

THE ECHO CHAMBERS

To him the gatekeeper opens. The sheep hear his voice, and he calls his own sheep by name and leads them out. John 10:3 (ESV)

What you hear you obey. What you listen to changes you. There is an echo chamber of the Spirit, a place of divine voices. Voices are the rulers of the heart. What you hear over and over possesses you and what possesses you converts you. Your children will be put into my echo chambers. Their destinies will be formed. I will release the sacred voices to begin speaking to them and formulate their ideas, their beliefs, and their divine convictions. The echo chambers will place the eternities into their minds. They will not lead with their egos. They will not conclude with their selfishness or partiality. Your children shall be blessed with the gift of divine ownership. They will own the divine, not borrow or rent it. Your children will succeed when others abandon. All this will be the fruit of the echo chamber of my Holy Spirit. I will sever from their minds the voices of death, deceit and self-worship. They shall hear my voice and follow no other. I will drown out all the voices of death. When they are faced with hard choices, they will easily know what to do. The hard parts of life will be easy for them. They will live outside the reach of life's tornadoes and hurricanes. No devastating storms for them. The echo chamber unmasks the source of every voice. A child who can hear me and repeat what I say is a medicine to the heart. Place my word before them day and night and it will echo into eternity.

TODAY I PRAY...

Jeremiah 29:11 over my children. The Lord has a divine and beautiful future for them. The plans God has for them are good plans of success and prosperity. My children will realize these plans and believe them and follow them.

...IN THE NAME OF JESUS.

THE SEEDS OF ETERNITY

"While the earth remains, seedtime and harvest, cold and heat, summer and winter, day and night, shall not cease." Genesis 8:22 (ESV)

Deep calls to deep. The seeds I have planted inside your children are not of this earth. They are not subject to wind, rain, flood, cold, heat or ice. Famine cannot destroy them. Harsh conditions cannot kill them. Pressures from sin, life, death or man cannot alter their divine purpose for existing. My seeds are infused with eternity. Every seed I have placed in your children is eternal. The eternal is permanent. Eternal desires cannot be drowned by the pleasures of this earth. They are permanent and everlasting, reaching from earth to heaven. Eternity is the heart of each seed. Explosive growth is their code. Unending bliss is their shell. These seeds are void of all decay, corrosion and natural fading. I am placing eternity in your children's hearts. I am impregnating their spirit with the pieces of heaven that they need to reproduce heaven in others. My seeds live. They breathe healing, spread happiness, restore life and replace the useless with the effective. These seeds germinating in your children will define them. These seeds will create their world-view, their personal convictions and their appetites for eternity. Your children are containers of indescribable beauties from heaven. Their gestures, tone of voice, beliefs, attitudes, choices, friendships and interests are all reflections of the seeds within them. These seeds will be passed on from generation to generation. Year after year, just as they were born from me, they will return to me.

TODAY I PRAY...

Romans 8:28 over my children. Because they love God and are called according to His purpose, God will work out all the situations of their life for their good. Situations that look bad will be worked out by the power of the Holy Spirit in their lives.

...IN THE NAME OF JESUS.

THE TASTE OF A SALTY SOUL

"You are the salt of the earth, but if salt has lost its taste, how shall its saltiness be restored? It is no longer good for anything except to be thrown out and trampled under people's feet." Matthew 5:13 (ESV)

I will give your children a salty soul. Their way of speaking and their way of loving will create avalanches of attraction. They will make the world thirst and hunger for me. I will salt their words and spice their personalities with love. I will cause them to know the secret parts of me. I will cause them to inherit the powers of divine influence. They will speak to the most powerful people on earth: life-altering men and women, controllers of countries, leaders of armies, and those who run the heart of nations. A salty soul is irresistible; it is filled with goodness and undiminished kindness. Their wisdom will be salted so when the mighty and influential inquire, their words will not be able to be rejected. They will paint pictures of love with their language. They will make lost people's hearts burn with hope and possibilities. Your children are the full meal, the appetizer and the main course. They are the dessert for those buried in the cold of starvation. Salt preserves and purifies. It creates thirst and it is valuable and indispensable. Everyone requires salt to live. The salt in your children will become like a chisel, chipping away at the stone that is around people's hearts. It will be a divine time of soothing the angry and betrayed and calming the tormenting fears of the night. They are the guardians of the embryos of life, the newly formed miracles that the naked eye cannot see. They are salting life, satisfying hungers, spicing reality and healing loneliness. A child with a salty soul is already delicious to me.

TODAY I PRAY...

1 Corinthians 2:9 over my children. Eye has not seen and ear has not heard the wonderful and amazing things that God has prepared for my children who love Him and want Him and desire Him and follow Him.

...IN THE NAME OF JESUS.

THE PERFECT NOTE LIFE

And when he had removed him, he raised up David to be their king, of whom he testified and said, 'I have found in David the son of Jesse a man after my heart, who will do all my will.' Acts 13:22 (ESV)

An untuned life sends the world into chaos. Untuned notes make all things unbearable. The untuned focus on minors. Untuned notes hurt the ears of the heart. Those untuned to me follow lies and confusion. They walk with death and partner with division. But I am tuning your children to myself. They will feel what I feel. They will perceive what I perceive. They will sing the songs I write. When the divine tuning takes place, the whole world sounds different. No more seditions in their mind, inner poisons or outward diseases. No more severity, abuses or betrayals. To be tuned to me is to never miss the perfect note life. The perfect note life is a life that I can live through. I can move freely through this life. I have total, complete control and freedom. There are no limits. The perfect note life has no shrills, screeching, whining or drama. The perfect note life fills the altars of heaven with nonreturnable praises. Worship is created by the actions of the perfect note. The perfect note life melts heaven with its perfect harmony with me. There are no different songs, notes, tunes or symphonies of life. The perfect note child is a perfect crescendo for my life songs. They speak my language. Their sound matches my sound. Their song harmonizes with my song. We become one note, opening heaven for the world to see.

TODAY I PRAY...

Proverbs 3:5-8 over my children. They will trust in the Lord will all their heart and will not lean to their own understanding. In every way they walk and every situation they face, they will trust in the Lord and not lean to their own insights and opinions, but will constantly acknowledge, follow, and obey Him.

...IN THE NAME OF JESUS.

THE GIFTED CHILD

As each has received a gift, use it to serve one another, as good stewards of God's varied grace... 1 Peter 4:10 (ESV)

"Unlimited" is your child's middle name. Gifted is your child's image. Loved is your child's mindset and humble is your child's inner life. With these gifts the gifted life will be born and released. The gifted child is a wonder, a miracle, an awe-inspiring reminder that I live in children. Their gifts shall create liberty for the changed mind. They shall create servants of healing and doctors of the heart. The gifted child will spread their wings and cover the world with my shadow. They shall stand tiny but loom large. They shall be a fireplace for the cold soul. A rocking chair for the weary. The gifted child hears with my ears. They speak my spirit-filled words and light the world on fire. Gifts make me famous; talents make you famous. A gift is a divinity given to a person with no natural talent in that area. The divinely gifted create believers out of unbelievers. They persuade the doubter, convince the skeptic and convert the atheist. A gifted child opens the eyes of the heart. Innocence converts fools! A child like yours is a miracle waiting to grow into their genius. Trust me with your children's futures. Cultivate your children's gifts, display me through them. A gifted child erases doubt and multiplies faith. When I want to reveal myself to the world, I choose a child and turn the heads of the lost.

TODAY I PRAY...

Mark 11:22-23 over my children. They will not be doubters. They will not be foolish unbelievers. They will say what the Word of God says and have faith that if they agree with what He says, they can speak to any mountain they face and any situation that comes against them, and that mountain will be removed.

...IN THE NAME OF JESUS.

THE DREAM CHILD

But, as it is written, "What no eye has seen, nor ear heard, nor the heart of man imagined, what God has prepared for those who love him..." 1 Corinthians 2:9 (ESV)

What you dream chases you forever! Dreamers are creators. They dream from their hope. They create scenarios of beauty. A God-dreamer is a child who lives inside my mind. To dream like me is to stand alone as an eagle in the presence of chickens. I dream in finished possibilities. Because I am unlimited I can only birth unlimited dreams. The dream child is fascinated by heaven. They occupy a body and have a soul, but they walk in their Spirit. Their flame is never extinguished. Their talk is springtime. Their eyesight is foresight and their heart is the same size as mine. They are ever-spreading healing vines. My mind is their medicine. They grow sinews of life and wrap the broken in them. Where there were skeletons, there are now masterpieces of creativity. Their dreams rename the past, redefine the labels, redesign the soul and recalibrate the mind of the heart. The dream child is a living contradiction of faith. Where there is no vision, the people disintegrate. Dreamers expel nightmares, unravel truth cures, and unwrap me. They serve me on a plate of possibility. They clothe the world in the spirit of yes! My little dreamers will recreate the world, minus the fingerprints of death. The child who dreams changes reality.

TODAY I PRAY...

Jeremiah 32:17 over my children. They will know that nothing is too difficult for God. There is no person He cannot save, no situation He cannot change, no blessing He cannot give them, and no miracle He cannot perform for them.

...IN THE NAME OF JESUS.

CHILDREN OF THE IMPERISHABLE

That their hearts may be encouraged, being knit together in love, to reach all the riches of full assurance of understanding and the knowledge of God's mystery, which is Christ, in whom are hidden all the treasures of wisdom and knowledge.

Colossians 2:2-3 (ESV)

All wealth is hidden in me. All treasure is defined by me. All things worth having are given by me. I am the essence of all incorruptible riches. I live to add wealth to you. It is my pleasure to give to you and your children. The worldly man seeks temporary treasures and will die trying to attain them. Those who do not live for the kingdom, waste their living pursuing what they believe will make them happy. Some find it, abuse it and die without hope. True wealth is anything born of me. Only what I birth and give away will stand the test of time. Your children will be children of the imperishable, that which life cannot kill, that which time cannot diminish, and that which cannot be spoiled, corrupted, defiled or ruined by man. The child of the imperishable is a divine creation. Your children will see through the fool's gold of life. They will not treasure what turns to dust, chase smoke, praise dirt or crave illusions. The child of the imperishable knows what true treasure is. Your children will surround themselves with the true riches of life: the love of family, the honors and wisdom of life, the powers of the Holy Spirit, the beauties of unbiased love, the knowledge of the holy, the kindness that heals, the mind at peace, the heart unbroken, the gratitude of life, home undiminished, faith unaltered, and the presence of my Spirit. These are the true treasures to which they will dedicate their lives. Success is the prosperity of unconditional love. The child of the imperishable will enter heaven with boatloads of true riches. A life lived in true wealth is a life of divine ecstasies, assurance, safeties and intimacies.

TODAY I PRAY...

Matthew 19:20 over my children, that they will be children of supernatural faith who have no trouble believing God for signs, wonders, and miracles. They will know that what is impossible for man, is possible for God. Their hearts will hold firm that our God is the God of the impossible.

...IN THE NAME OF JESUS.

CHILDREN OF THE SWORD

For the word of God is living and active, sharper than any two-edged sword, piercing to the division of soul and of spirit, of joints and of marrow, and discerning the thoughts and intentions of the heart. Hebrews 4:12 (ESV)

Children of the sword cannot be defeated! Their sword skills are their power. A child who masters the sword of their destiny is unstoppable. Every choice a child makes forms their sword. The children of the sword are masters of my word. My word is eternal, inextinguishable, powerful, healing, milk, bread and meat. My word is life, light, rain and seed. My word is living, active and life altering. A child of the sword learns the secrets of my word and the power of using my word to defeat self, conquer enemies and define life. All health comes from the word. My word is a mirror and a hammer, it is fire in the bones and incorruptible seed. By my word, I hold the universe together. All things that are life are in my word. My Son is the word seen. Children of the sword are masters of revealed and divine truth. They walk inside my living and electric revelation. Night never touches them, fear runs from them, and they wear their sword on their heart. Its power is irresistible; its abilities are absolute, its rule is complete, and its insights are life-changing. My word is living, moving and breathing inside your children. It will lift them to the highest places of honor and power. Children of the sword have no unanswered questions. I speak and they obey. Perfect obedience produces perfect results.

TODAY, I PRAY...

Jeremiah 1:12 over my children. He is watching over the promises that He has given them, to perform those promises and to make the covenant of those promises come true. They will be known as children who stand on the rock of His promises and are unmoved and unshaken by the tragedies and brokenness in the world.

...IN THE NAME OF JESUS.

WHERE WOUNDS DISSOLVE

For I will restore health to you, and your wounds I will heal,
declares the Lord, because they have called you an outcast: 'It is Zion, for whom no
one cares!' Jeremiah 30:17 (ESV)

The world is wounded and speaks from its pain. It hears from its torn soul. It responds from unresolved fear. It is covered in insecurity and lives in apprehension and timidity. It ponders failure, eats disaster and meditates on terror. Not so for your children. I am making your children a place where wounds dissolve and a place of divine penicillin where the infections of life are healed, and the oozing poisons are cleansed. Your children are born to be healers, living hospitals, walking medicines, and permanent remedies. They will be divine solutions and not problems, cures and not diseases, answers not questions, and divine appointments not disasters. Your children will carry within them the powers to heal the broken hearted and the knowledge to lead the blind out of the darkness. They shall be deliverers of the oppressed, lighthouses of truth, filters of mixed truth and they shall call out of the darkness the wandering, aimless people. They will see those who wander like zombies. Your children will see the hidden wounds and pour in the medicine. They will rage against the wounds that cripple the souls of the world. They will be life givers, truth tellers, wells of hope, fire brands of purpose. They will know the way to the hospital where wounded hearts are mended. A heart that can heal, heals a soul that can mend, which mends a mind that can think like me and arrives at the place where wounds dissolve and infinite wealth lives.

TODAY I PRAY...

Hebrew 4:16 over my children. They will run to the Throne of Grace. They are habitually addicted to finding their help in God and not outside of God. In Him, their day will be filled with the divine, they will perceive it and live beyond their present circumstances.

...IN THE NAME OF JESUS.

THE SMILES OF GRACE

And my God will liberally supply (fill until full) your every need according to His riches in glory in Christ Jesus. Philippians 4:19 (AMP)

Grace is unmerited favor wrapped in divine sufficiency. Grace is where mercy is the umpire. Grace is the best for the least, at no cost. Grace is divine influence upon the heart reflected in the life. Grace is victory triumphing over sin. Grace is the power to be what you cannot be. These are the smiles of grace that will be reflected in your children's lives. Grace smiles at failure because it knows it will win! Your children will be clothed in the smiles of grace. They will be the most forgiving, tolerant, and patient people. They will be the carriers of grace, wrapping the unworthy in worthiness, the failures in victory, the lost with eyes, the deaf with ears and the hurt with comfort. They will be the first to not abandon or forsake people. With your children, the sinners will find a friend, the rejected will find acceptance, and the unwanted will find loving, nurturing arms. These are the foundations of those touched by grace. Troubles flee in their presence and fear runs away. True grace is the life of generosity, giving to those that do not deserve it, and forgiving those that can never earn it. The smiles of grace change the landscapes of the defeated. Grace places man at the victory side of Calvary. Grace gleans life from the hopelessness, befriends the despised, and transforms the hard hearted. Those smiles of grace will be the permanent state of your children.

TODAY I PRAY...

Psalm 91:2-3, 10 over my children. They will dwell in the secret place of the Most High and will abide in the shadow of the Almighty. No evil will befall them and no plague come near their dwelling. They will be safe inside the hiding place of God.

...IN THE NAME OF JESUS.

THE WONDERS OF THE INVISIBLE

By faith he left Egypt, not being afraid of the anger of the king, for he endured as seeing him who is invisible. Hebrews 11:27 (ESV)

There is a life very few get to experience, a life beyond this known realm. A life lived in and from the other side. The side where angels tread, where sin is dead, and sorrow flees away. A place of continual sunshine and a place where there is no pain, hurt, grief, or tears. A place of unapproachable light, where no fear can walk, and no dangers lurk. There is a life you and yours can live, a place where I live. In this place, there is no terrorizing, miseries, insanity, lame, wounded or mutilated, deformity, hate, racisms, brokenness, criminals, or liars, cheaters or abusers. There is life on the other side. The invisible place where the saints sing, and old age is no more. Here is where your children will behold the wonders of the invisible. Where I live on the other side, there is no wars, bondage, trauma, snakes, dragons, predators, prisons, or jails of the soul. Your children will live here. They will travel back and forth between this life and where I live. They will take spiritual journeys and the invisible realities of my home will become the tangible place of true love, faith and hope. The invisible contains the tangible. Faith will be their chauffeur. It will guide them to the room of miracles where the impossible becomes the normal, the unbelievable becomes the achievable and the unimaginable becomes the possible. Your children are being purposed for the greatest journey of their lives where there are no limits to their dreams, and they can rest inside the shoes of wonder.

TODAY I PRAY...

Psalm 27:4 over my children that they will be the kind of children that desire one thing above all things: that they may dwell in the House of the Lord. They will behold the beauty of the Lord and meditate in His presence all day long.

...IN THE NAME OF JESUS.

EMPOWERED FROM ON HIGH

"But you will receive power when the Holy Spirit has come upon you, and you will be my witnesses in Jerusalem and in all Judea and Samaria, and to the end of the earth." Acts 1:8 (ESV)

Power is the unleashing of me, the event of my presence, and the sound of my voice. Power is my irresistible force relocating tragedy and my invisible hand-removing the visible hand of the serpent. Your children will be supernaturally powerful. They will walk in a flame of wonder-working power. To have this power, your children will live between sacred upsurges and downturns, where I will remove things and add better things and where I will sever relationships and replace them with more meaningful ones. I will cut and close the issues of their hearts. Sacred upsurges produce divine abilities. I remove a piece of them and add a piece of me. I am power and I cannot be challenged, defeated, threatened or minimized. I am a total, all-consuming power. I am the scythe. I gather strength and pour it into the hearts of your children. No more anguish or agonizing sleep. Your children will come back to life. They will experience deep, satisfying healing power. I only create masterpieces. I only create divers that go to the deepest places in my ocean. Power recreates the world. Power children have tasted the spices of prayer, the fruit of self-sacrifice and the pains of self-denial. Your children will turn the world upside down.

TODAY I PRAY...

2 Timothy 4:18 over my children. The Lord will preserve them and protect them and keep them safe from all evil people. He will protect them from evil designs and the strategies of their enemies. They will walk with confidence and supernatural assurance in their hearts. Their eyes will be filled with the fires of purpose.

...IN THE NAME OF JESUS.

CHILDREN OF THE WELL

With joy you will draw water from the wells of salvation. Isaiah 12:3 (ESV)

I unstop the wells and clear out the dirt. I unplug the clogged wells of salvation and command the waters to flow. No trickles or tiny streams, but only free flowing wells of fresh water. This water quenches the spiritual thirst of the nations and is so satisfying that men and women will come from all over the world to find it. They shall rush up to my mountain and flow up the hills. They shall come from every tribe, tongue and kindred. All people of all languages shall long for the water from the wells. Your children shall have direct access to these wells. They shall find them, dig them and drink from them. The children who discover my wells are never thirsty again. They are not food for predators or wood for deadly fires of the soul. Your children shall remain encased in the wells of salvation. The children of the well will never be weed eaters, mud farmers or cowards of faith. Your children will open rivers where there are deserts and fountains where there are snake pits. The children of the well open rivers for the starved and those dwelling in famine. No intellectual thirst for deaths ideas, cultivators of laziness, altars of vanity, or uneatable truths will be found where the waters flow. Your children will wade in the waters of eternity. They will unlock the wells of salvation for the thirsty masses. Wherever this water can be found, people will arrive. Water brings hope!

TODAY I PRAY...

Ecclesiastes 3:1-3 over my children. They will be aware of the leadings of the Holy Spirit and of the timing of the Holy Spirit. There is a time to plant and a time to uproot. There is a time to bless and a time to withhold blessing. There is a time to give and there is a time to withhold giving. They will be children of divine sensitivity, knowing the ways and the timings of God.

...IN THE NAME OF JESUS.

THE SACRED PEARLS

Again, the kingdom of heaven is like a merchant in search of fine pearls, who, on finding one pearl of great value, went and sold all that he had and bought it.
Matthew 13:45-46 (ESV)

There is only one pearl of great price and that is my Son. He is the field. He is the price. He is the reward and He is the pearl. Give everything to have this pearl. Find it, polish it, save it, own it, love it and give it away. Lead your children to the pearl so that they will be pearl polishers. The pearl shall light the way for them to walk. They shall be architects of divine value. Their hammer will be their sanctified will and their nail shall be their divine choices. They shall change the old lamps of truth with the light of the pearl of ultimate price. They shall give the pearl and others will become wealthy with God. The pearl eradicates soul poverty, brain parasites and heart infections. The pearl's value is absorbed by loving the pearl. It heals while it is being loved, valued and worshiped. A life without the pearl is a life of rubbish collecting, mudslinging, and cheap choices. He who tries to make something sacred out of something cheap twists the face of God. The pearl builds a firm place to stand. It changes fates, heals personalities, reforms the wretched, and transforms the cruel and criminal parts of the heart. This pearl resurrects love in all its dearest forms. When the pearl takes residence in your heart, it becomes your children's true and most valuable inheritance. The choirs of heaven begin to sing. Sadness leaves forever. The soul finds its harbor and the spirit wanders no more. Embrace the pearl with your children and feel heaven's favor and pleasure.

TODAY, I PRAY...

Galatians 5:22 over my children. They will be full of the fruit of the Spirit. They will be full of love, joy, peace, goodness, gentleness, self-control, humility, faithfulness, and long-suffering. They will perfect these fruits in their lives and spend their lives giving away these fruits to those who have nothing.

...IN THE NAME OF JESUS.

DRINKING PASSION

Jesus stood and said in a loud voice, "Let anyone who is thirsty come to me and drink. 38 Whoever believes in me, as Scripture has said, rivers of living water will flow from within them. John 7:37-38 (NIV)

A soul without passion is in a funeral procession. Your children are born for divine passion. To be possessed by divine passion makes you a walking, consuming fire of light. Divine passion is the spark that lights the path of your children's destiny. A child with wrong passions becomes a disguise of the world. A child with demonic passions becomes a scourge of the family. Drinking divine passions heals the sicknesses of life. Man is a wandering black hole, full of unidentifiable emptiness. When your children begin drinking Godly passions, all the divine explosions will happen. They will love truth, be addicted to integrity, live a disciplined life, and be sensitive to my Holy Spirit. Goodness, kindness and gentleness will take over their behavior. Passion purges, breaks the mold, and will defy the odds. Your passionate children will outdo every natural living creation. Veil after veil will lift. They will become slaves of the light, managers of the lamps of heaven, healers of unseen needs, and menders of broken nets. Their life will be hidden in Christ, revealed in Christ and sustained by Christ. They will end the death dances of the lost. Their ship will never see destruction. They shall always see the lighthouse of heaven. Drinking divine passions removes corrupt passions and starts an inner culture revival, where the blind see and the hungry are fed. Start drinking the passions of Christ, my Son, and be found divinely possessed by love.

TODAY I PRAY...

Genesis 28:15 over my children. They will have a desire to find their Promised Land. They will not allow anyone or anything to stop them from achieving that goal. They will know they do not walk alone, but the Lord holds their hand, drives the enemies out of their land, and leads them right into the center of their Promised Land.

...IN THE NAME OF JESUS.

THE RHINO'S SKIN

Being strengthened with all power, according to his glorious might, for all endurance and patience with joy; giving thanks to the Father, who has qualified you to share in the inheritance of the saints in light. Colossians 1:11-12 (ESV)

The rhino's skin is impenetrable by predator's teeth and snake's fangs. It can tolerate abuse, attacks and assaults. Your children shall be thick skinned and tenderhearted. I will train your children to endure hardship and prosper in it. To be unmoved by verbal abuse and be promoted in it. When I am ready to promote you, I will send someone to offend you. If you love him or her, you will activate a promotion. If you don't, you will activate a retest. When I am ready to change you, I will ask you to do something you fear. These are the insights of the thick-skinned and tender hearted. Your children will be trained in the school of eternity's longevity, not callousness or hardheartedness, but divine toughness. A child who can identify the sources of human behavior will never be a victim of the imperfect. They shall never wander between pains, get stuck or hurt, or create ruts of unforgiveness. Your children shall have an ever-flowing river of love, because they are unaffected by offenses, rudeness, cruelties and abominations. They shall never fit in the devil's mold. They are my clay, my vessel to form, and my trumpet to tune. Know this, no person, circumstance, or amount of abuse shall separate me from them and them from you.

TODAY I PRAY...

Deuteronomy 11:24 over my children. Wherever the soles of their feet tread shall belong to them. They will be conquerors of the Promised Land and find their inheritance. They will spend their whole lives learning how to give it away to all who are poor. They will give life and give love in abundance.

...IN THE NAME OF JESUS.

INDISPENSABLE

Fear not, therefore; you are of more value than many sparrows.
Matthew 10:31 (ESV)

Your children will never be throwaways. They will never have the secondhand touch. They will always be indispensable to me. Their mark is loved, cherished and honored. I need who your children will become. I have created a place of divine achievements for them. There are no replacements for them. They are and always will be indispensable. They are a love story in the making. They have no limitations in my eyes. They are a miracle being discovered. They are the fruit of all my grace, the result of all my love, the destination of all my power and the story of Calvary's victory. They hold within them, the living, incorruptible seed of life. They are a song of preserving health. There are no mutating viruses of unbelief; no germs, diseases or bacteria of fear breeding in them. I set them apart and separate them from the agitating fears, moral conflicts and irritating pressures of life. Your children are tattooed on my arm. Their names are engraved on my heart and their faces are carved on the palms of my hands. I can't live without them. Ignorance is their enemy. Preserving, healing, saving and loving is their code of honor. I will open heaven's windows and send down showers of refreshment. I will put a fire in their bones and my word shall always be on their lips. They will never be lost. They shall see with their eyes of faith and hear what others cannot. They are indispensable always and forever to me.

TODAY I PRAY...

Joshua 10:24 over my children. They will find the giants in the land, drag them out of their strongholds, place their feet on their neck in victory, and hang them high for all to see. They will have a life that is giant-free.

...IN THE NAME OF JESUS.

WAITING TO BE MADE WINE

Then your barns will be filled with plenty, and your vats will be bursting with wine.
Proverbs 3:10 (ESV)

Your children will be like crushed grapes ready to be made into wine. Masters of delight, experts at healing, mentors of the blind and wounded, none of your children will be permanent victims of life. They shall be raised by me, through me and for me. At an early age they will begin to grow their wings of destiny. Divine crushing will produce the divine abilities of flight, fight and might. They shall spend their lives giving out barrels of unconquerable hope to those that are self-judged, self-hated and self-rejected. They will be givers and creators of new wine; new healing powers will flow through them. New eyesight, vision, perspective, perception and lives will be ruled by divine conclusions. Your children will not be afraid of my divine ways. They will not run away from the divine processes of my Holy Spirit. They will honor. They will crave transformation and embrace the sacred places of change. Yes, they will live in expectancy. They will live waiting to be made the wine the lonely can drink, to enter the road of divine encounters, and to be the divine appointment the world is waiting for. Release the potential of their divine self. Mix the ingredients of grace, love and faith. Churn them and separate the precious from the worthless. Be their wine taster and see the world crave the wines of their lives.

TODAY I PRAY...

Joshua 13:1 over my children. They will know that whatever they achieve, whatever goals they reach, whatever blessings they obtain, there still remains much more land to be conquered in their life. God will always increase them.

...IN THE NAME OF JESUS.

45

THE TRANSFORMATION COCOON

You are my hiding place; you will protect me from trouble and surround me with songs of deliverance. Psalm 32:7 (NIV)

I am placing your children in my transformation cocoon. I am weaving and adding the divine. I am wrapping them in new undiscovered graces, voices and attributes. New convictions, perspectives, vitalities of fire, abilities of discernment, and powers of deduction are being birthed in them. I am giving them the power to instantly separate the vile from the precious, the lost from the found, and the truths from the lies. They shall walk on a different path then their friends. Their path will have no laziness, empty pursuits, or carnal curiosities. They shall have a perfect heart towards me. From week to week, you will see them grow and adjust into my image. They will embrace my ways at an early age. The fork in the road will never be a challenge to them. They shall be clothed in the fear of the Lord. They will run towards me in their inner thoughts. Their secret and private meditations shall heal and guide them to the oasis of change. My transformation cocoon is the place of protection. Change is how they stay away from the grip of darkness. He who changes towards me is never attracted to the candies of darkness. Change keeps your children accessible to my life-giving presence. The seeds of ruin die in the hands of change. They will be made rescuers of the unwanted, unloved and forsaken. The beautiful angels guard the divinities of the redeemable soul. Good change kills bad change. Prepare for a lifetime of unexpected surprises.

TODAY I PRAY...

Exodus 3:6-8. That my children will know that the Holy Spirit is leading them to a land filled with milk and honey, filled with the grapes of the Promised Land, the blessings of the Promised Land, and the territories of the Promised Land. They will not spend their lives pursuing things that are worthless and without eternal value.

...IN THE NAME OF JESUS.

THE UNPAYABLES

That I may know him and the power of his resurrection, and may share his sufferings, becoming like him in his death, that by any means possible I may attain the resurrection from the dead. Philippians 3:10-14 (ESV)

A selfish heart always demands the highest price. I am making your children heart surgeons, repairers of the brokenness of the human race, and destroyers of the selfish gene. Those with the selfish gene love the benefits of grace, but they throw away the rewards of the Calvary life; They surrender the blessings of being crucified in Christ. The selfish have forgotten the eternal. They have been conquered by the immediate and possessed by the powers of instant gratification. They are lost in self-preservation and wounded by convenience. The selfless life brings the rewards of the invisible treasuries of the victories of Calvary. What is worth the most is a life lived in the heart of the unpayables. What you do that you do not require payment for is divine. Your children shall be the children of the unpayables. Their life shall be free from the torturous chains of enslaving needs, tormenting wants and vexing unfulfillable desires. The selfless child builds a life that Satan cannot manipulate. The selfless child gives before they take, offer healing before they ask to be healed and do for others before they ask for help. The selfless child is the trophy of love. Their heart looks like an open hand, not a grasping hand. The selfish give away their true wealth: the ability to need nothing, want nothing and be beholden to no one. He who does not need anything is invincible.

TODAY I PRAY...

Isaiah 26:3-4 over my children. They will know that those who confidently trust in the Lord will be kept in perfect peace and be untroubled by the trials of life, by the scary situations going on in the world. They will maintain their position of peace.

...IN THE NAME OF JESUS.

THE FIRES OF THE ETERNAL

If I say, "I will not mention him, or speak any more in his name,"
there is in my heart as it were a burning fire shut up in my bones, and I am weary
with holding it in, and I cannot. Jeremiah 20:9 (ESV)

Fire is the cleanser and purifier of the human heart. A life without the eternal fire fades into obscurity. I am sending the holy fires to your children and my fires will consume them. Holy desires will drive them into my arms; their whole life long. I will possess their souls with holiness and compel them with love. All foreign desires will die in the presence of the eternal and shapeless shadows will flee away. The Philistines of false tradition will explode into pieces that cannot be salvaged. Their longings, aches, compulsions, urges and wants shall all match mine. Do not worry about their future. Like the pillar of fire in the wilderness, I will keep them safe. I will keep them safe like the flaming sword in the garden. I will protect their eternity. The fires of the eternal are seldom found, seldom known and seldom pursued. Your children are children of the fire. Only the eternal will attract them and consume them. They shall live free from the vile and barbaric. The touch of anarchy will pass them by. Their inner culture will sizzle, boil and run over with purities. They will see no despair, loneliness, futility, apathy or lethargy. You will hear the magnificent roaring of a Lion of Judah in your home.

TODAY I PRAY...

2 Kings 2:9 that my children will know as they follow their mentors and fully engage in their training and education as sons and daughters of God, they will receive a double portion of miracle-working power.

...IN THE NAME OF JESUS.

THERE IS A PLACE

As an apple tree among the trees of the forest, so is my beloved among the young men. With great delight I sat in his shadow, and his fruit was sweet to my taste. Song of Solomon 2:3 (ESV)

There is a place that I have made where miracles are born. A place where sorrows die and snakes shrivel up. A place where dreams are made and destines found. A place where the lonely are turned into warriors, the sick are made well, emptiness is cured and shadows die. There is a place where the sound of divinity rules the soul, the shadow of death dies, and the cold and frigid heart is warmed. There is a place where tears are turned to laughter, defeat to victory, fear to faith and where the orphan finds a father. There is a place where I wait for my children to come to me and fall into my arms. Here, disease is burned out of the soul, the wicked mind is cured, insanities die and the mind is put at ease. Yes, there is a place where the hopeless mind is cured and where the broken heart can sing again. There is a place for the abandoned to find a home, the fearful to be released, the chains to melt and the grip of death to be loosed. Yes, come now! Bring your little ones to the place where medicines are made, wholeness sings, beauty thrives and inspiration is born. Come now, bring your little ones to that place where you and I are alone, talking, hearing, sharing, giving, receiving and seeing how the whole world changes. There is a place alone with me where all of life is a well.

TODAY I PRAY...

Isaiah 40:2-3 over my children. They will know that for any unhappiness, discouragement, or misery they experience, God will give them a double portion of unstoppable, irresistible, inexhaustible joy.

...IN THE NAME OF JESUS.

THE ART OF DIVINE ADJUSTMENTS

"Father, if you are willing, remove this cup from me. Nevertheless, not my will, but yours, be done." Luke 22:42 (ESV)

Divine adjustments fix life's mistakes. When you stop being adjustable, your journey ends. I am sending you some adjustments and things you need to change. Adjustments are needed in your mindsets, attitudes and desires. Every adjustment opens a door of opportunity. Your children will be given the gift of adjustment wisdom. There will be no soul prisons or shriveling hearts for them. They will not be slaves to fear. They shall adjust their way to me. They shall be filled with the enchantments of pleasing me. In your family, there will be no lost causes, hopeless cases, twisted loyalties, or forsaken convictions. Adjusters never permanently lose. You cannot defeat someone who refuses to quit. Your children's gift is to adjust their lives to light. They are light dwellers, light bringers, and light eaters. Every divine position of blessing requires a divine adjustment. When you adjust, you release mercy. Children followed by mercy know the power of repositioning. Those that are able to adjust see where God is going and follow. They hear what God is saying and do it. They feel what God wants and fulfill it. No judgments, disasters, or tragedies are headed their way. The adjusted see the stop sign. They feel the changes in the wind. They are never victims of the changing seasons of life. I will train your children in the art of divine adjustments and wherever I am, there shall they be also, safe, useful and matchless.

TODAY I PRAY...

Job 42:10-12. My children will know that as they pray for their friends and their enemies, that God will give them back twice as much as anything they lose or that was taken from them. They will receive twice as much as they had before and spend their lives with their hands filled with the blessings of God to give away to the orphan and widow.

...IN THE NAME OF JESUS.

CONTENTMENT DIVINE

Not that I speak in regard to need, for I have learned in whatever state I am, to be content: Philippians 4:11 (NKJV)

Contentment is the perfect aligning of God with the soul and spirit. He who is divinely content lacks nothing. A content child is desperate only for me and for my will for their lives. Divine contentment is to be enhanced perfectly by love. A dissatisfied child becomes food for predators. A content child is satisfied with what I provide. Complaining is how a person tells me they don't trust my plan for their lives. Many mind and soul predators will approach your children, but because they are fully satisfied with me, they will not bend the knee to the counterfeit contentment of life. Your children will not crave the lap of Delilah. They will not wallow at the pool of despair; the eyes of forbidden fruit will not hypnotize them. They will not long for the wealth of the flesh and the riches of the world. Your children will be happy and complete. The longing of their souls will be fully met in me. They will not be driven by the void of an unloved soul or captured by the false illusions of dreams. They are the chosen, future priests, healers, comforters, teachers, authors, singers and entrepreneurs of the kingdom of heaven. All divine contentment is eternal. There is no temporal in eternity. I will translate myself to them. I will break myself down one divine piece at a time. They shall not spend their lives fighting the void or beating the air. Their hearts are perfectly focused. The satisfied see clearly because they are full and whole. Only the empty are for sale.

TODAY I PRAY...

James 1:27 over my children that they will be practicers of pure religion and they will spend their lives rescuing orphans and widows, taking care of the poor, and not participating in the carnal worldliness of life. They are choice vessels of the will and the wonders of a good God.

...IN THE NAME OF JESUS.

51

WHERE GOODNESS FOLLOWS

Surely goodness and mercy shall follow me all the days of my life,
and I shall dwell in the house of the Lord forever. Psalm 23:6 (ESV)

Goodness comes from goodness. Goodness is born from receiving undeserved love, kindness and mercy. The victims of goodness always pass it on. Live where goodness follows. Goodness in a child is a sign of the presence of divinity. A child filled with goodness lives in the embrace of uncommon favor. Heaven remains unlocked to them. They don't require the key, for they are the key. They are addicted to healing people through acts of mercy. Mercy is the right hand of goodness. A good-hearted child is headed for an ocean of love. Goodness is God inside of a child flowing out into the world. Goodness is the cure for a sick world, healing one person at a time. Goodness comes from vertical living. Vertical living is the pathway to being good hearted. Your children will live at the feet of goodness. They will erase the damage done to the victim. They will discover the atlas of my life. They will feast at the table of significance. Their names shall be famous for making me famous. They will be conductors of the healing waters of encouragement. They shall sit in the chair of value and consume the manna of heaven. They shall prevent the slaughter of the innocent, the abuse of the helpless and the rejections of the unloved. Theirs will be a life of divine announcements, proclamations of wholeness, declarations of acceptance and invitations of true unbiased happiness. No nightmares for the good-hearted, just heavenly dreams of delivering the oppressed of the world. Goodness is a reward for forgiveness.

TODAY I PRAY...

Over my children Habakkuk 3:19, that they will have the feet of a mountain deer and will be able to walk in places of great trial, stress, and difficulty without feeling it and without stumbling over it.

...IN THE NAME OF JESUS.

THE SCHOOL OF DIVINE CHOOSING

I call heaven and earth to witness against you today, that I have set before you life and death, blessing and curse. Therefore choose life, that you and your offspring may live... Deuteronomy 30:19 (ESV)

The divine chooser learns the power of unwanted circumstances. The divine chooser fears the powers of sowing and reaping. The divine chooser has learned from history's teachers, which life is worth living and which life brings death, destruction and misery. Bad choices are the fool's gold. Choices in the hands of a wise child bring great rewards to the whole family. All choices breed destinations and create consequences. There are no meaningless choices. Your children will learn the secrets of choosing. I will teach them the ability to identify the source and the root system behind a choice. I will give them the gift of identifying masks, deceptions, illusions and control tactics. Your children will enter the school of choosing. Right choices create unpolluted destinies. A right choice silences Satan. A right choice builds an impenetrable fortress of truth, which no evil can break through or lie can germinate. The essence of the fortress of truth can be honored, empowered or embraced. Right choices will be the armor of your children. What you choose converts you. Choosing divinely results in being placed in front of my throne. Your choices proclaim your intentions. Your choices reveal your future. A child trained in divine choosing has already won. You can rest in peace if your children choose the divine. No traps, disaster, wasted years or tuneless living will come to them. A house full of divine choosers is an invitation for me to come and live.

TODAY I PRAY...

Luke 10:39-41 over my children, that they will be the kind of children that choose the good part of life which, is sitting at the feet of Jesus. I declare that my children will listen to His teachings, His wisdom, and make wise decisions to follow and obey the will and plan of God for their lives.

...IN THE NAME OF JESUS.

THE ARCHITECT'S CHILD

Train up a child in the way he should go; even when he is old he will not depart from it. Proverbs 22:6 (ESV)

I am the architect designing your child's destiny. I only create geniuses of truth. As their architect, I will design their height, width and depth. I will put all the doors to their secret places in the right locations. There will be no wasted walls or unnecessary rooms. Everything they need, I will provide. I will give them: The perfect personality, one that heals by simply being near them; the perfect heart, large enough to fit the hurting world; and the perfect mind, clear enough to solve the spiritual questions of the world. They will receive a perfect soul, one full of compassion, that never ages or quits. They will always be able to feel and remove the pain of those they meet. They will be the perfect color, reflecting the beauties of unbiased love. All your children need will be theirs. Their perfect foundation will be unbreakable and unmovable. They will be able to withstand the storms of life: all shaking earthquakes, lightning, rain, flood and wind. I will be their divine covering, their perfect roof. I will protect them from the rains and hail. They will be perfect windows that let me in and let me out. Be at peace, for I am building, designing, stabilizing and painting a life lived in motion. I am providing for them movable divinities, edible realities and eternal convictions. Your children are stairs, not clouds. They are my intentional beauties and my purposeful creations.

TODAY I PRAY...

Revelation 1:17 over my children, that they will see Jesus in their lifetime and will have divine visitations from Him. They will encounter Jesus and fall at His feet many times in their lives. He will lay His right hand upon them, empowering them to display His glory, and saying, "Do not be afraid, for I am the Alpha and Omega and you have nothing to fear."

...IN THE NAME OF JESUS.

METAMORPHOSIS

But we all, with unveiled face, beholding as in a mirror the glory of the Lord, are being transformed into the same image from glory to glory, just as by the Spirit of the Lord. 2 Corinthians 3:18 (NKJV)

Allow the process of metamorphosis to transform you into me. Allow me to eclipse your doubts, overpower you with my love, and awaken you to wise living. I am leading your children to taste heaven, eat revelation and absorb truth. Pray these things. Cast these things like a net around your children, and watch them prosper beyond your ability to measure, for I am their height, width and their depth. There will be no shallow places in your children. There will be no winter, withering, or death for them. Nothing can freeze them when they are exposed to the chilling, cold-hearted world. They will not be hardened under unfairness or abuse. Your children are a place of revolution in all areas: inner, spiritual, ethical, social, and financial. They will be a place where divinity is absorbed and realized. They will be devoured by grace and night cannot touch them. The voice of tragedy cannot speak to them. They will not walk on the platform of failure. They are explosions of divine thought, bombs of insight and destroyers of the terrorists who take life. Metamorphosis is the act of becoming, the place of seeing, the inner call to come up higher. In metamorphosis, in that instant in time, nothing meets everything.

TODAY I PRAY...

Isaiah 52:8 over my children. They will be known throughout the land and world as bringers of good news. Their feet will be blessed wherever they walk in this world, because they bring good news to discouraged and brokenhearted people.

...IN THE NAME OF JESUS.

THE LESSONS OF PAIN

Surely he has borne our griefs and carried our sorrows; yet we esteemed him stricken, smitten by God, and afflicted. Isaiah 53:4 (ESV)

Pain makes people selfish, self-absorbed and weak. Fear, self-doubt and panic can strike the heart. Pain will make you a monster or a minister, bitter or better; it is a choice. The wise management of all forms of pain is crucial to the survival and the thriving of your family. Pain can tear lives apart or bring them together. Know this, I will teach your children the skill of transforming pain into power. Your children will be powerful soldiers who build walls of comfort around their friends and family. Their ears shall not grow sick with the hearing of pain. They shall be an ocean of healing truth and healing ways. Wave after wave of comfort shall flow from them. I will embrace them with mirrors of truth. I will surround them with mountains of faith and direct them with the lights and lamps of a transparent heart. They will encounter no blind alleys, ruts of stubbornness, or wood of the flesh that can ignite the flames of deadly passions. Your children are painkillers. They will erase the song of the devil in the heart's of the lost. They will become a pain shield, a reflection of wholeness, and a reaction of health. Yes, your children are learning the lessons of pain from my perspective. The stars are not dead, the heavens are not locked, the virtues still exist and the pains are subsiding. They shall live in my orchards picking the fruits of healing and stopping time by healing time.

TODAY I PRAY...

Numbers 13:30-33 over my children. They will be like Joshua and Caleb, who went to spy out the Promised Land and came back with a good report, saying, "Let us go in and possess the land from the Jordan to the sea, for we are well able to conquer the giants in the land." This will be their confession, their proclamation, their lifestyle's declaration.

...IN THE NAME OF JESUS.

PURCHASED WITH GOLD

For you were bought with a price. So glorify God in your body. 1 Corinthians 6:20
(ESV)

I purchased you with my life. Perfection entered corruption and opened a door for redemption. The house of the dead was healed. The graveyards were opened and the dead souls became the living hope of the world. Since the beginning of time, while you were still in the womb, I was weaving the golden thread of grace and love into your future. I was putting selfishness in prison. I am making your children the caretakers of my gold, the managers of my divine nature and the directors of my soul's resources. They will be rich, humble, powerful people who own the keys to my storehouses. They will be revealers of the secrets of Calvary, possessors of good, and divine fortresses with divine impulses. They will be addicted to making the sick well, walking with worthy hands and sanctified feet. They will be gold, pure, incompatible gold. They will walk in pleasant places, on paths made of butter, on roads paved with my nature, and on viper-less paths where enemies are massacred by holiness. Your children have had their destinies paid for. Use these truths as your prayer weapons. Use them to disarm corruption, falsehood and criminal hearts, to rip the masks off the wolves and to raise your children at my feet. Your children are breakthrough children. They can win when all others lose. They will dwell in certainties, thrive in the rich storehouse of purities and sleep in the bed of a clean conscience. The price will call out the gold.

TODAY I PRAY...

Daniel 6:20 over my children that even though they're surrounded by ferocious, loud predators and intimidating people, they will be like Daniel in the Lion's Den and pray to God. He will shut the mouth of the lions and quiet the intimidations of the people in power.

...IN THE NAME OF JESUS.

BUYING THE FIELD

The kingdom of heaven is like treasure hidden in a field, which a man found and covered up. Then in his joy he goes and sells all that he has and buys that field.
Matthew 13:44 (ESV)

Invest in the eternal and you will never steal from yourself. There is a field, a place of becoming, a place of identity, a field of life where you must educate your children on the value of the divine life. Help them strengthen their appreciation for the eternal. He who loves the cheap, loses the sacred. Your children will invest themselves in my field, my places of divine exchange, where I take poverty and give the true riches of life. To buy the field is to give yourself for my divine purposes. Your children will be eternity's children. They shall feast at the table of divine truths. There shall be no flies or cobwebs of the mind. They will not experience empty storehouses or lack anything. There will be no tortured expectancies or lack of divine rest. They shall rest in their field: plowing, sowing, cultivating and reaping the blessings. They will pursued by blessings, chased by good fortune and made owners of the eternal. Your children shall reap where they have not sown and they shall be apostles to the poor, evangelists of grace and pastors of lost souls. Their field is a fruitful, full of pomegranates, grapes and rich, thick goodness. Their field shall provide for thousands, feed thousands, heal thousands and rescue the orphans of the world. The field is worth more than all other earthly treasures for its greatest treasure is me!

TODAY I PRAY...

Matthew 9:17 over my children that they will be the kind of children who never hold on to old wineskins of truth, but constantly turn in their old wineskins and receive from God the new wine of divine revelation. All the days of their life, they will be in the center of God's will and contribute to the revivals God does all over the world.

...IN THE NAME OF JESUS.

THE ETERNAL GRAPES

...and every branch that does bear fruit he prunes, that it may bear more fruit.
John 15:2b (ESV)

Your children are the tenders of my vineyard. They are called by me to make the healing wines of Zion. Every flavor of wine they make heals the broken-hearted. Every taste stirs up revival. They make new wine from my table. Their feet are sacred feet. They are born to soothe the aching soul and to mend the soul that has been ripped open by cruelty's hands. Their love will enlarge the heart, expand the spirit and cultivate expectancy. No doubters will be in your house. There will be no permanent unbelief, wavering or double-minded souls. Your children are arrows of conviction. They are focused, simple, wise and sanctified. The enemy comes and finds nothing in them. They shall be trained and prepared for the eternal grapes, the grapes I eat. Everything eternal is indestructible. Every piece of me is an eternal wine. Place these in your children and they will become divine, divine carriers of revelation truth. They will be driven from loss and embraced by heavens wealth. Let my wine linger upon them, lead them to the grapes, teach their palette to love the taste of illumined truth, and they will always be chased by freedom. Comfort them with heaven's kind of reality, a reality based on faith and miracles, not logic or natural facts. I hold the universe together with my word. I promise you I will hold you and your family together as well. Your children will never be food for predators. They are fruit evangelists. Those who win souls with divine truth, sacred insights and healing revelation feed on eternal grapes and make your world a heavenly dream.

TODAY I PRAY...

Over my children Proverbs 3:10, that the vats and storehouses of God will belong to my children. The wine will overflow the vats and the grain will flow all over the ground and floors of their family, their children, and their grandchildren. Their lives will be full of new wine revelation and the wheat of blessed harvests.

...IN THE NAME OF JESUS.

THE RICHEST PLACE OF ALL

In him lie hidden all the treasures of wisdom and knowledge. Colossians 2:33 (NLT)

Your children will live in heaven's inextinguishable love. They will always hear the call of Utopia, the place where I dwell and the place of divinity's perfections. They will not linger at the door of emptiness. They will not build their future on the movable sands of compromise. Their lives will be built by Calvary's victories. Theirs will be a life of divine riches. A rich mind will guide them, a tender heart will keep them near to me and a wise discernment will preserve them until my coming. Rest in your faith. Drink the nectar of divine sincerity. Rest on the pillow of a clear conscience and reach your faith. Reach for the untasted riches of Utopia's call. I will surround you like a wall. I will encompass you with confidence. I will fight for you with fierce contending. You will tread on the head of the serpent and stop the beating heart of fear. Trust me morning, noon and night. Rely on my voice to guide you in raising and influencing your children. Throw a parade for Utopia's call, the call to the perfect place, heart, and love. Know this, your children will erase the tragedies of life from the rejected, unwanted, unloved people of the world. They will do this from a hidden place of communion with me. From this place they will go to the battlefields of victory. Your offspring will sing Utopia's call.

TODAY I PRAY...

Deuteronomy 11:14 over my children. They will receive the latter rain and the former rain. The former rain will soften the soil of their heart for the planting of the seed and the latter rain will make the seed grow and prosper. They will gather in the corn of the Word of God, the wine of the Word of God, and the oils of the healing of the Holy Spirit.

...IN THE NAME OF JESUS.

WHEN SPRING COMES

For behold, the winter is past; the rain is over and gone. The flowers appear on the earth, the time of singing has come, and the voice of the turtledove is heard in our land. Song of Solomon 2:11-12 (ESV)

When spring comes to your children, the withering vanishes and the dead and dying are gone. Spring calls out to the holy seeds, "come forth, bloom, bloom and bring forth life." Love directs the storm. Love controls the budding. Love calls out to the nothingness, "arise and shine." The spring has started for you and your family. It is time to be chased by hope, captured by faith and conquered by love. There is no rust in the soul, breakdown of joy, or interruptions of momentum. Instead, there is growth, life, and divine rivers of expectancy. The winter is over, now the infusions of my nature begin. Your children will begin to bring forth the blossoms of their genius. The introductions to wholeness take over. Faith creates capability. Originality is born. Individuality raises its voice, defines its purpose and creates its platforms for your children. It's time to dance the jigs of spring! Death is gone, life is here. Perfect timing will be the crown of your children's soul. There will be no unnecessary journeys, detours of distraction, lost time or wasted dreams. Perfectly well thoughts will guide their choices. Their thinking will be love locked, faith led, and truth-possessed. This is their springtime. Let the sounds of growth be heard in your house. Build on hope and drive in the nails of victory. Let the atmosphere release the fragrances of new birth.

TODAY I PRAY...

Ephesians 3:20 over my children. They will know without any doubt in their hearts that God will do exceedingly, abundantly above anything they ask or pray and they will not waiver in double-minded unbelief. They will be convinced of the mighty, miracle-working power dwelling within them and become the conduit of God's greatest blessings for others.

...IN THE NAME OF JESUS.

IN DIVINITY'S BALANCE

Finally, brothers, whatever is true, whatever is honorable, whatever is just, whatever is pure, whatever is lovely, whatever is commendable, if there is any excellence, if there is anything worthy of praise, think about these things. Philippians 4:8 (ESV)

Balance is the ability to maintain perfect equilibrium of faith, love and truth. This will be one of your children's gifts. Divine balance creates safety in the face of danger, sure-footing in the storms of life, reasonable reactions, safe emotions during emotional earthquakes, longevity of relationships, covenant thinking that releases covenant fruits, and the power to release the fountains of well-being. Your children's future has already been paid for. Rest in assurance, sleep in the lap of faith, and let love form you. I will place in them a voice that will shake the world. True balance is true health. It is all of me, divinely fed to all their appetites. This is the place of immunity, the untouchable place where evil cannot walk. I will make them capable masters of the divine. They will never lose the substance of heaven for grasping at shadows. They will graze on balance and be strong in all areas. They will be knowledgeable of me. They will be filled with diversity, loving everyone without bias. No taste of bitterness will ever make a home in their hearts. They will always have all they need, to find me, love me and know me.

TODAY, I PRAY...

Philippians 4:19. My children will know that God will supply all their needs according to their riches and glory that abide in Christ Jesus. And to the measure that Jesus has everything, they will have everything.

...IN THE NAME OF JESUS.

THE SACRED ADDICTIONS

As a deer pants for flowing streams, so pants my soul for you, O God. My soul thirsts for God, for the living God. When shall I come and appear before God? Psalm 42:1-2 (ESV)

Trust in my intervening power. I will always rescue your children. If you spend your life rescuing other people's children, I will always rescue yours. Through sacred addictions, heaven is realized. A sacred addiction is the inner life of the Spirit. I will teach you the power of sacred addictions. A child that is addicted to me will hear, feel, touch, know and sense me. Sacred addictions create divine tangibility. Sacred addictions place your children in divine positions of unchallengeable faith. They will be found in places where they can absorb me and step through the veil and touch the unimaginable ecstasy of intimacy with me. A sacred addiction is an eternal possession, where stability and unending discoveries are found. A place where the mind is totally directed by Holy Spirit. Sacred addiction is normal Christ-like living. Your children will never need memory healing, heart surgery or the healing of soul cancer. When you lead a child to sacred addictions, you set them free from the corrupting, corroding influences of lies, deception and counterfeit faiths. Your children will have hearing ears and searching hearts. They will paint the path to me. All sacred addictions erase the fingerprints of Satan. Live addicted to truth, for a slave of truth is the only truly free soul there is.

TODAY I PRAY...

Romans 5:17 over my children. Because of the abundance of grace that rests on them, they will rule in this world and they will reign over the temptations and burdens this world lays on people. The wonderful blessings of God's Spirit will be upon them.

...IN THE NAME OF JESUS.

THE ANCHORS THAT HOLD

We have this as a sure and steadfast anchor of the soul, a hope that enters into the inner place behind the curtain. Hebrews 6:19 (ESV)

Not everything called security is secure. Not everything known as stability stabilizes. Not everything called safe is safe. But there is an anchor that holds through every storm of life. It will hold through every forsaking, rejection, betrayal and circumstance you will ever meet. I am the only true anchor. I am immovable. I cannot be bullied, controlled or manipulated by anyone. I am eternity wrapped in perfect kindness. I am love in action and goodness on display. I am the mountain too big to move. I will be your children's life anchor. I will teach them to walk within the meaningful, to dwell within the rhema life, and to be enclosed by beauty's face. Their life will be a steady one, washed in truth, stabilized by insights of truth, and immunized by faith's touch. The anchor that holds will be their hiding place. They shall possess the heart of wonder. Absolutes will guide them. Variables will flee from them. The old coat of the unbeliever and the old worn out shoes of poverty they shall never wear. Rats shall never invade their minds for they shall be rich in mind and wealthy in soul. The anchor that holds will be their life's torch. They will have no confusion, vexation or active living torment. Peace, confidence and the power of divine satisfaction will make their home in them. And through everything, their anchor will hold!

TODAY I PRAY...

Mark 4:20 over my children. They will be the kind of children that receive 30-fold blessings in many areas of their life, 60-fold blessings in many areas of their life, and 100-fold blessings in many areas of their life.

...IN THE NAME OF JESUS.

THE DOORWAYS OF HEAVEN

I am the door. If anyone enters by Me, he will be saved, and will go in and out and find pasture. John 10:9 (ESV)

Heaven is full of doors; these doors lead to destinies, divinities and connections to me. Very few people have found these doorways. They are a secret known only to the trustworthy. These doorways lead to all the knowledge and treasures of the universe, and to the hope of human kind. Each door opens a universe healing knowledge. Your children shall be guardians of the secrets of heaven. If it were not hidden, mankind would misuse this knowledge and life's answers would be changed by man's greed and vanity. Your children will know who I really am and they shall reveal me to the world. Power, influence and wealth shall be theirs. These things will be wrapped in generosity and humility. They will be free from materialism, self-promotion and empire building. The doorways will heal poverty, cure infirmities, release destinies, save the lost and guide the blind to the eternal lights. They shall be the watchmen on the towers of Zion. They are called, chosen, anointed and equipped with all that is me. Take your time with them, nurture their nurturing nature. Love them to the entrances of eternity.

TODAY I PRAY...

2 Chronicles 20:20 over my children. They will walk in the fear of the Lord and believe His saints, His prophets, and His teachers all the days of their lives. Because of this, they shall be honored, promoted, and given great levels of divine prosperity.

...IN THE NAME OF JESUS.

THE CONQUEROR'S CROWN

The one who conquers will be clothed thus in white garments, and I will never blot his name out of the book of life. I will confess his name before my Father and before his angels. Revelation 3:5 (ESV)

I will place the conqueror's crown on the head of your children. From the crown of thorns comes the conqueror's crown. Your children are already appointed their victories. They shall be chefs of the feasts of healing. Their victories shall lead them and follow after them. Victory will be their middle name. Their appetite will grow with the touch of clarity. Their self- control will produce the fruit of kindness. Their character will be the visible banner that they are untouchable by evil. They shall live unrivaled, unchallenged and unbreakable. They shall be filled with the incontestable knowledge of the intimate disciple. They shall hate worthlessness and cherish the divine. These are my promises to you. Your children shall possess the heart of an explorer. Their discoveries will be wholeness, pricelessness and royalty. They shall understand the lows of my Spirit and the secrets of the divine life. They shall endure no wandering in desserts or wasted years pursuing vanities. They will not have skeleton souls. They shall worship piece by piece, glory by glory, light by light and cure by cure. I alone will be there favorite flavor. Their attitude will be designed by my life. Their demeanor will be a reflection of the place they dwell. Love will always draw them from the poverties of life into the paradise of knowledge. This is the conqueror's crown they shall pursue and wear forever!

TODAY I PRAY...

Psalm 119:32 over my children that they will have a heart the same size as God's heart: a heart of love, mercy, compassion, long-suffering, goodness, and purity. They will not have a selfish heart of rebellion, unbelief, deceit or fear.

...IN THE NAME OF JESUS.

THE LIVING PRODUCE

But those that were sown on the good soil are the ones who hear the word and accept it and bear fruit, thirtyfold and sixtyfold and a hundredfold. Mark 4:20 (ESV)

I am placing an anointing on your children to produce resurrection life. Everywhere they go, they will be like overflowing wells. They will live in the overflowing place of my Spirit. They shall never experience famine of Spirit or the drought of the disobedient. Your children shall touch dead and worthless things and turn them into springs of hope. They shall speak and rivers shall appear where deserts have occupied the soul. Your children are producers, creators, and inventors. Wealth shall flow their way, like a river wild. Their warfare will be the eternal war against poverty, suffering and pain. T555555555hey will live to eradicate them from the earth. I am placing an eternal seed inside them, so they will believe only what I say. They will declare a thing and I will do it. There will be no scraps for them or for you. They will not experience fragmented grace, only feasts of love. They will find no trash, only treasures; nothing worthless, only the priceless; and nothing broken, only the whole. Yes your children shall fill ten lifetimes of storehouses and ten lifetimes of good will. Tortured memories and twisted ideas will not be theirs. They will experience only the sweet wine of commune with me and not sour grapes. They shall sit at my table and have their fill of me. Their memories will be full of miracles. They will have a past filled with victories and a future possessed by the sound of the trumpets of victory. They will rest in this knowledge and sleep in my arms. All will be well. The living produce, grow, and advance.

TODAY I PRAY...

Psalm 42:1-2 over my children. As the deer panteth for the water brooks and streams of God, my children will be thirsty for God and hungry for God. All the days of their life, they will be desperate for the things of God and pursue Him without hesitation or looking back.

...IN THE NAME OF JESUS.

I AM THE ALL

And he is before all things, and in him all things hold together. Colossians 1:17 (ESV)

I am your all in all. I fill heaven and I fill you. I am your source and your resource. I give without greed. I impart life where death has ruled. I am perfect and complete sufficiency. I am what you need as a parent; what you lack I possess. I am the bread your children need to grow into divine geniuses. They will possess exceptional intellectual powers. They will dissect me with their divine lights. Their lamps will open their minds to my mind. They will see from behind the veil of my presence. None of my children shall taste the bread of idleness. They shall rise like eagles from the ashes around them. They shall fly when others crawl. They shall be spokesmen for me. They shall fight the enemies of freedom from shore to shore and sea to sea. I shall anoint them to hear what the wise man hears, see what the seer sees and know what the surrendered know. Be at peace. I am the all. I am the I am. I am everything you and your children will ever need. Lean on my word, feed on my truth, dance in my victory and let me be your all in all!

TODAY I PRAY...

Romans 4:18-22 over my children. As Abraham did not stagger in unbelief at the promises of God but gave glory to God and was persuaded that what God had promised, He was able to perform, my children too will be like him. They do not stagger or waver at the promise of God. They are persuaded, convinced, and cast out all abiding doubts from their mind.

...IN THE NAME OF JESUS.

THE DEBT PAYER'S HEART

By canceling the record of debt that stood against us with its legal demands. This he set aside, nailing it to the cross. Colossians 2:14 (ESV)

You will spend your life reducing, erasing and eliminating the debt of other people's souls and hearts. Your children will be debt eradicators. A debt is a pit of guilt, a grave of futility, and a coffin of hopelessness. I paid every debt of your mind, soul, life and heart. I hate all forms of debt. Debt is the mountain of unpayable mistakes that this world carries. It drowns in it. Its hope is smothered by it. You will be taught the skill of destructing debt. This divine ability will grow like an oak tree in your children. You are raising debt demolishers. You are raising children that discern the debts of the soul and whose eyes see pain and remove it. Your children's spirits will commune with me, hear me and see me. A child raised to tear down mountains is invincible. A child who can hear guilt and remove it is divine. A child with a debt-destroying parent is already a healer. You are the debt-payer. You are the immunity spreader. You solve the impossible and you erase the uneraseable. You cure the cancer of guilt and the rabies of the mind. You silence the madness in the masses you reach. Remember, your children are a living, evolving potential of goodness. You hate debt because I hate debt. I paid what you could never pay. I forgave what you could not repent for. I set you free form the load you could not carry, now pass it on!

TODAY I PRAY...

Genesis 39:1-6 over my children. They are like Joseph who found favor everywhere he went and with everyone he was around. He had favor with his teachers and employers and he was promoted to the highest places of influence and power. My children will be promoted and prosper in everything they do because the hand of God is upon them.

...IN THE NAME OF JESUS.

THE BEAUTY THAT FOLLOWS YOU

Let the favor of the Lord our God be upon us, and establish the work of our hands upon us; yes, establish the work of our hands! Psalm 90:17 (ESV)

It is beauty that follows you when you follow me. You are an artist of beauty for your children. Your life is one lived in constant transition. You go from beauty to beauty. I am beauty absorbed. I will give you the steps to follow to make your children lovers of divine beauty. They will not be attracted to the false and fake beauty of the world. They will not surrender or succumb. They will be divinely equipped with the powers to resist carnal passions, false temptations and negative pressures. They shall dress in the virtues of Calvary and wear the shoes of the redemption gospel. They shall wear a gold nature, a purple robe of favor and the helmet of humility's victories. Your beautiful children will be chased by a beauty not of this earth, not hand-made, man-made or self-made. Their beauty shall attract the lonely heart and capture the souls of the seekers of truth. Yes, you are a creator of beauty. It does follow you everywhere you obey. The beauty I am will become the beauty they crave. The beauty I reveal comes from total surrender. The beauties of Calvary cannot be read, they must be poised by pursuit. Every child possessed by beauty never wants anything else. Be the beauty you wish your children to seek.

TODAY I PRAY...

Psalm 1:2-3 over my children. Their delight will be in the Law of the Lord and in His Law, they will meditate. They shall be like trees planted by the rivers of water. They will bring forth their fruit in their season and their leaves shall never wither. They shall never participate in beliefs, ideas, religions, or any kind of philosophy that is full of worthless, untrue ideas.

...IN THE NAME OF JESUS.

THE RESTED SOUL

For I will satisfy the weary soul, and every languishing soul I will replenish.
Jeremiah 31:25 (ESV)

To descend is to ascend. To rest is to create years of divine work. The absence of divine rest opens the doors of the cannibal attitudes. Rest relieves stress and heals the overload. Divine rest is faith working while the body is rejuvenating. The rested child learns, acts, hears and does better. The poisons of unrest reshape the soul with the barbed wire of torment and fear. The child of rest knows the secrets of self-refreshing. They understand the balance between work and rest, the secret of a revitalized spirit. I will bring them to the place where souls relax and lose their tortured imaginations. I will keep them emotionally happy. I will remove unending labor and heaviness from them. Worry will not take root in their inner life. Come to me and I will be their refuge. They will take my easy yoke and learn from me. They will be lovely in heart and be ruled by gratitude's embrace. My presence will be with them and they shall not eat the bread of anxious toil. They shall receive the gift of sweet, divine sleep. They shall love the solitary place of communion with me, which is a place of recharging. They shall not fret, worry or have the touch of fear on them. They shall dwell in safety and reap unexpected harvests. I will satisfy their soul in drought and their bones shall be made fat with health. They shall become a place of flowing streams where the weary souls will be made new. Their language will be uplifted by their strength and they shall know the laws of replenishing. They shall not faint or grow weary in well doing. They shall wait upon me and find their oasis of rest.

TODAY I PRAY...

Joshua 1:8 over my children that the book of the Law will not depart out of their mouth. They shall be confessors of the Word of God, expounders of the Word of God, teachers of the Word of God, and prophets of the Word of God. They shall find great prosperity and great success because their life is founded on the beliefs of the Word of God.

...IN THE NAME OF JESUS.

THE FRUITFUL LIFE

I am the vine; you are the branches. Whoever abides in me and I in him, he it is that bears much fruit, for apart from me you can do nothing. John 15:5 (ESV)

I am the giver of fruitful life. I am the source of the abundant thick and ripe branches of divine fruit. Divine fruit is developed through Christ-likeness. Fruit is the face of digested seeds and the only reliable judge. Whoever bears good fruit knows me. I am the fruitful life. I will lead your children to a life of unending fruit bearing. I will create their divine root system where they can drink deeply from the healing waters of life. I am the true vine they will love. They will learn the secret of abiding. They will enjoy the tilling of their soil. They will drink in the sunshine and feed on the minerals and vitamins of fellowship. They are the purveyors of the fruitful life. Only fruit matters, everything else is empty air. My command upon them is to be fruitful and bring forth life daily. The fruit of my Spirit will be their strong tower. Love shall define them, joy shall fulfill them and peace shall protect them. Patience shall preserve them, kindness shall heal them and goodness shall restore them. Faithfulness shall inspire them, gentleness shall surround them and self-control shall sanctify them. They are the fruitful life in the making. They shall carry virtue, knowledge and steadfastness. They shall ask whatever they want and I shall do it. They shall spend their lives glorifying me through decades of fruit bearing. All their lives they shall make everything they touch fruitful.

TODAY I PRAY...

Luke 6:38 over my children. They will receive so many blessings that God will press them down and shake them together. Their blessings will flow out of their lives as if my children were a river of God's heavenly supply for the starving people of the world.

...IN THE NAME OF JESUS.

THE BLESSED LIFE

And all these blessings shall come upon you and overtake you, if you obey the voice of the Lord your God. Deuteronomy 28:2 (ESV)

The blessed life is a life hidden in the place of divine intimacy. To be blessed is to be given the armor of immunity. The blessed child shines with the radiance of favor and preferential treatment. Your children shall be a blessing magnet. They shall draw blessings to themselves. They shall absorb the favored places of life. They shall trust me and lean on me for wisdom. They shall fear me and appreciate me. I will supply all their needs according to my riches and glory. I shall only give them the richest blessings, not used or second hand experiences. Only the best will be given to them, pressed down, shaken together and running over. Their cup shall never stop overflowing. I will keep them and make my face shine upon them and be gracious to them and give them peace. They shall not fear or be dismayed. I will lift my countenance upon them and give them rest. I will never leave them or forsake them. They will abound to every good work. All their lives will be spent in service to the needy and orphaned. I will lift them up and keep them safe from evil men. I will hold their hand and lead them to the promised land. It shall go well with them. They shall inherit health and prosper financially. Their barrel of flour shall never run out. I will set them on high above the fallen natures of men and my blessing will overtake and possess them. They shall ooze with fullness. They shall be followed by goodness and mercy and see the salvation of their family and friends. Their ways will please me and I will make even their enemies to be at peace with them.

TODAY I PRAY...

Romans 15:13 over my children, that they will be filled with hope. A joyful expectancy will run their lives, that something good is about to happen. The spirit of hope will live inside their hearts and they will be known for having joyful, good expectations. All day long they will have an expectancy that good things will be done unto them by their Heavenly Father.

...IN THE NAME OF JESUS.

THE GOODNESS CURE

I believe that I shall look upon the goodness of the Lord in the land of the living!
Psalm 27:13 (ESV)

The goodness cure dissolves the touch of tragedy. Goodness is a life emptied of revenge. Goodness is a life in total harmony with me. I am good and I love to do good. I make people addicts of goodness. I drive badness away. I expel evil, meanness and disfavor. I am the goodness of life. Anyone near me becomes good. To know me is to know goodness. Goodness dissolves the fingerprints of cruelty. It is the medicine of the soul. Good people love me. Know this, that goodness shall chase and catch your children. They shall dwell in the hand of goodness. Good fortune shall be theirs. Good days, good people and goodwill shall never abandon them. They shall dwell in my house as heirs and be made rich with provision. I will build storehouses of goodness for your children. They shall taste my goodness and feel my kindness. They shall eat heaven's fruit and be baptized in goodwill. They shall be loved in the household of faith, loved by the sinner and the reject. They shall be kept healthy and fed. I will keep their lives in the hollow of my hand. Good seasons shall be theirs and satisfy the desires of their heart. They will call and I will answer. They will abide in the cocoon of favored love. My steadfast love will never depart from their door. I will make my goodness to pass before their eyes and they shall tie themselves to it. They will dwell in my courts and be satisfied with my house. They shall shout and the walls of sorrow will fall. They shall dance on the enemy's plans and move many from disaster to goodness. They shall continue to say that the Lord has been good to them.

TODAY I PRAY...

Nehemiah 8:10 over my children that the joy of the Lord will be their supernatural source of strength today. Because they have joy and have mastered the art of accessing joy, they will not be depressed or moody or given to negative thoughts or emotions. They will be filled with the spirit of joy all day long.

...IN THE NAME OF JESUS.

THE FOUNTAIN OF YOUTH

...who forgives all your iniquity, who heals all your diseases, who redeems your life from the pit, who crowns you with steadfast love and mercy, who satisfies you with good so that your youth is renewed like the eagle's. Psalm 103:3-5 (ESV)

Loving keeps you young and in a place of continual youth. I will reveal it to your children. I will teach them the secrets of longevity and youthfulness. They shall have access to my fountain of youth. The secrets of love keep the heart young and joyful. Joyfulness and a merciful heart are a continual feast. Forgiveness keeps death from the bones and mercy keeps hope alive. Truthfulness renews the divine senses. Encouragement is a tonic of self-healing. Those who dwell in faith live for many years in the hands of fearlessness. All who honor me are given love, honor and long-life. The consistently obedient are chased by blessings daily. Those who heal the sick receive healing. Those who forgive the unforgivable are kept free from the bitterness of life. A soldier of spiritual hunger never loses their spiritual passion and maintains their divine passions. These passions hold the emotional predators of life at bay. Your children shall always remember my blessings. I will heal their diseases and renew their youth like the eagles. I will crown their years with loving-kindness. I will keep them from the destroyer and open the fountain of renewing. I will keep the windows of heaven open and rebuke the devourers. All tears will be wiped away and darkness shall flee. The springs of the water of life will be theirs without payment. I will dig springs and open rivers and they shall swim in the midst of the river of life. They shall still be bearing fruit in their old age.

TODAY I PRAY...

Psalm 41:11 over my children. God favors my children. All of their enemies, internal and external, will be defeated before their eyes. They will be children who know how to use their spiritual weapons and walk in victory over their enemies.

...IN THE NAME OF JESUS.

THE ARMOR OF PRAISE

I will sing to the Lord as long as I live; I will sing praise to my God while I have being.
Psalm 104:33 (ESV)

Praise silences the enemy's voice and opens the windows of heaven. Sincere praise heals the atmosphere and makes room for my restoring presence. Praise is the automatic response to holiness and love. Praise is the original purpose of mankind. Those that choose to praise me redesign themselves. Praise recreates the DNA of mankind. Those that habitually praise habitually reign. Praise is the sound of a heart finding God. Praise is the sound of a life in touch with heaven. Praise is the reality of God inside the heart. Praise connects men with saved realities. Praise is the response of the human heart to the absence of fear, failure and defeat. Praise shapes the face of God to fit in the heart of mankind. Praise is the sound of a person realizing the victories of Calvary. When you praise, you release the invisible realities of heaven. Praise will be the permanent state of your children's heart. They shall praise their way through life and conquer as they go. They shall tear down the walls of Jericho. They shall rip open the windows of heaven. They shall fill the halls of heaven with gratitude's crown. Your children will be filled with all my fullness. They shall live in constant fulfillment. Joy and gladness shall mark them. The fruit of their lips shall open all the doors of destiny for them. Heaven cannot say no to praise. Expect that your children walk with me in heaven while inhabiting earth. Praise will define them and keep them at the foot of my throne, dressed always in the armor of praise.

TODAY I PRAY...

Romans 8:37 over my children. They are more than conquerors through Christ Jesus. My children will not barely get by, but will reign and rule and thrive in this life. They will be filled with victory over their personal emotions, over their mind, over relationships and circumstances, over their social, spiritual and personal life.

...IN THE NAME OF JESUS.

THE FLOURISHING

The righteous flourish like the palm tree and grow like a cedar in Lebanon. They are planted in the house of the Lord; they flourish in the courts of our God.
Psalm 92:12-13 (ESV)

I will command the spirit of flourishing to come and rest upon your children. It shall cause them to be outrageously generous and selfless. Their abundance shall lead them and make them paymasters on the earth. They shall build homes for the orphans and cover the widows of the earth in safety. They shall nourish the starving souls of the earth and be a storehouse for the malnourished children of the world. The spirit of flourishing shall remain in them until their last day. From the branches of their tree, many shall come and find refuge. I will be with them everywhere they go. They will habitually succeed. Though their beginning may seem slow, their end shall be great. Be patient while the buds bloom and bloom and bring forth fruit.
The fragrances of heaven shall rest upon them and they shall fill the tabernacles of the earth with the prosperity of heaven. They shall have an abundance of peace, flourish in drought and thrive in famine. They shall flourish like the palm tree and be like the cedars of Lebanon. Their vineyards shall grow into acres of grapes and vines. Their vines shall be thick and heavy with the grace fruits of my Spirit. There shall be no deserts in their soul and no waste places in their minds. They shall be an ever-yielding orchard of divine life, flourishing and blossoming into life eternal.

TODAY I PRAY...

Psalm 23 over my children that the Lord is their Shepherd today and because of that, they shall not want for anything in their lives. The Lord will lead them to green pastures and still, flowing waters. The Lord will be with them when they pass through any fear and make their cup run over. He will prepare a table for them in the presence of their enemies. He will lead them in the path of righteousness for His Name's sake. Goodness and mercy will follow them all the days of their lives.

...IN THE NAME OF JESUS.

THE TRUTH SLAVE

...and you will know the truth, and the truth will set you free. John 8:32 (ESV)

The only truly free person is a slave to truth. Freedom is born in the field of uncorrupted truth. When the mind becomes engulfed in the flames of truth, a liberator is born. All the wealth of truth depends on the truth you embrace. Truth keeps the fingerprints of Satan off of the soul. All failures come from insulting the truth. The truth slave cannot betray his conscience. Therefore, he becomes a shield for the Spirit. The truth slave is on a road to completeness. Every aspect of the divine nature can only grow into maturity when fed truth. Trust is the armor around heaven. Truth is the enforcer and designer of the boundaries of belief, the incubator of miracles, and the womb of reality. Truth is the antibiotic for all of the diseases of the crooked soul. Your children shall be champions of truth. They will enter my mind, explore its infinity and come forth with lightning bolts of life altering truth. One truth kills a thousand lies. Your children shall cherish the divine truth. It will be their paintbrush and their gravel. Truth is a reliable judge. They shall have truth be the tuner of their souls. Truth exterminates lies, rules foolishness, defines me, reveals love, opens divinity's door and colors the world with reliable beauty. It delivers the captives, saves the lost, deflates fear, and rescues identities. It defends the light, armors the mind, exposes darkness and empowers the divine. Truth equips the weak, reinforces heaven, protects the helpless and unmasks the wolf. All truth shall be your children's creed and code of ethics, always and everywhere.

TODAY I PRAY...

Isaiah 26:12-14. My children will not be terrorized by any overbearing person. They will have the ability to handle people with the grace of God and the wisdom of God. They will be so full of grace and love and goodness, even the worst kinds of people will love them and they'll have a ministry to people no one else can reach.

...IN THE NAME OF JESUS.

THE PURE IN HEART

Blessed are the pure in heart, for they will see God. Matthew 5:8 (NIV)

The pure in heart see me. The pure in heart only have one master. They are single-hearted and feed on the light. Truth, justice and reality are their weapons, their swords and shields. The pure in heart dwell in honorable places. Justice is their clothing. They seek to harm no one. They think on things sacred, lovely and of good report. They are allergic to all that defiles, harms, corrupts or damages. Only what is worthy of heaven is allowed authority in their hearts. The praise worthy attracts their attention. Your children shall have clean hearts, untouched by the spiders and spider webs of hypocrisy. They shall be famous for having an excellent spirit. The child of purity lives without fences, for they are a fence unto themselves. They have no red lights because they know by nature where to go, when to stop and when to yield. Their obedience to the truth will purify their souls and authenticity shall rule their choices. Their pure heart comes with all the virtues they need to live above life's temptations. The deceitfulness of sin shall never rule them. The cares of the world shall be like smoke, a vapor that disappears. Only the undefiled will summon them. They shall be examples of godliness in speech, character, ethics and attitudes. Their convictions shall be unmovable. The pure child is not for sale!

TODAY I PRAY...

Psalm 27:1-4 over my children. They will be led by revelation light and when they are surrounded by overwhelming feelings, they will run to Jesus, their Rock. They will stand strong and firm and full of faith and hope.

...IN THE NAME OF JESUS.

THE NATURE OF HEAVEN

Through these he has given us his very great and precious promises, so that through them you may participate in the divine nature, 2 Peter 1:4 (NIV)

To obtain my nature is to end the inner wars. My nature is the perfection of love, the completeness of truth, the beauty of holiness and the fullness of faith. A child dressed in my nature becomes a weapon of heaven. I am the hope of your children. I know their battles and their tendencies. I know their DNA. I know where the twists and turns of their journey are located. I feel their frustrations. I hear their silent voice of fear and the whispers of their hearts. I am fully acquainted with their uprisings and their times of discouragement. I will be there for them always. I rescue them from my nature in them. My nature is my presence. Wherever my nature is my presence is. My nature is the death of that carnal fed Adamic, sinful self. I will weave my golden threads into your children. Every piece of me in them unifies to me. I partner with myself in them. I trust myself; therefore, I hear myself and answer you. My nature ruling in your children is the sure unbreakable guarantee of victory and success. My nature is the flawless part of anyone flawed or broken. What they cannot achieve, I can. Where they give up, I do not. Where they faint, I keep going on. My nature is the essence of all of heaven and your children are the containers of eternity in a small body. The entire universe, with all its powers, lives inside your children.

TODAY I PRAY...

Deuteronomy 28:2. The blessing of the Lord will pursue my children all day long. They will be chased by the blessing of the Lord. They will be possessed with the blessing of the Lord. They will be distributors to everyone of the blessing of the Lord. They are blessed every day for the rest of their lives.

...IN THE NAME OF JESUS.

THE THINGS THAT SCAR

He went to him and bound up his wounds, pouring on oil and wine. Then he set him on his own animal and brought him to an inn and took care of him. Luke 10:34 (ESV)

From the scars, come the trophies of love. The things that scar are the true dangers of the jungle and the wild, ferocious beasts. They are the animalistic appetites of the regions of hell running wild, seeking whom they may devour. It is the things that wound and rip and scar the soul that I will teach your children to mend. The things that scar are the fallen pieces in man: rage, pessimism, anger, fear, lust, greed, unfaithfulness, bitterness, malice, hate, deception, lying, stealing and killing. These are the lords and masters of death and the enemies within each unsaved person. The person who places their eternal future on unproved or disproved beliefs is a true creator of death. The things that scar must be starved, managed, mastered and repelled. Your children will heal by bringing healing to others, for healed wounds become medicine. Healed pain makes everyone ministers of cures. The one who loves, when he is scared, mocks death, cruelty and abuse. I heal the broken hearted, and so will they. I bind up the wounds, so will they. I close the bleeding heart, so will they. I bear the sins of the world and they will point people to me. I restore, heal and resurrect the cells of the failing heart. I bring back the outcasts. I pour in the oil and the wine and restore the wounds of the world and so will they.

TODAY I PRAY...

Psalm 37:8 over my children. They will taste and see the Lord is good and 'blessed is he who trusts in the Lord'. My children will love the personality of Jesus, the commandments of Jesus, the ideas of Jesus, the vision of Jesus, the purpose of Jesus, and the person of Jesus. The world will not satisfy because they will be satisfied with Jesus all the days of their lives.

...IN THE NAME OF JESUS.

FULLY PROTECTED

But the Lord is faithful. He will establish you and guard you against the evil one.
2 Thessalonians 3:3 (ESV)

I will be a hiding place for the heart from the shadows of death, for he who dwells under my wings sings. I will be a refuge from the storms of life. I will deliver your children from trouble. I will set them in a safe place and hide them in the cleft of the rock, so they are unreachable by evil. I will keep the demons out of their sleep. I will snap all the traps. The fowler will not catch them. The deadly sicknesses will not invade them. I will cover them with my winds. They will not fear the terrors of the night or be afraid of evil tidings. The deadly verbal arrows that fly by day shall not strike them. I will hide them in the secret place of my presence from the conspiracies of man and the strife of contentious people. No evil shall befall them or evil come near their dwelling. I will show them my salvations and satisfy them with long life. No weapon will work against them. They will be immune to damage. I will keep them as the apple of my eye. I will be a very present help in times of trouble. I will preserve their lives until I return. They are fully protected.

TODAY I PRAY...

Psalm 91:13 that my children will tread upon the lion, the adder, and the dragon. The lion represents intimidation and they will tread upon all intimidation trying to come into their life today. The adder poisons and they will tread on anything poisonous to their walk with God or to their personal development and identity. They shall tread upon the dragon, a figment upon their imagination that does not exist. They shall dominate their imagination and bring it into subjection under the Word of God.

...IN THE NAME OF JESUS.

THE WISE CHILD

But the wisdom from above is first pure, then peaceable, gentle, open to reason, full of mercy and good fruits, impartial and sincere. James 3:17 (ESV)

A wise child avoids the tragedies of life. They have an understanding of human nature and can detect danger and avoid it. The wise child walks in discernment. They are perceivers of the unseen and unsaid. They see within the masks and veils of man. The wise child does not believe what they are told. They believe the fruit they see. Wisdom from above is pure, without human bias. It is full of peaceful language and actions. It is full of gentleness and heals with its personality. It is an expert of reasonable behavior and full of merciful actions, not greedy, selfish or vain. My wisdom is full of the power to bear good fruit. It is impartial in its favor. Pure motives define it and it is ruled by sincere love. The wise child knows that wisdom is more precious than jewels and nothing you desire can compare with it. Long life is her reward. Riches fly to wisdom and honor possesses wisdom. The ways of a wise child are filled with divine pleasures and perfect pleasantness. All their paths are made of butter and oil. The wise child honors time and maximizes their time on earth. The wise child sits at the feet of understanding. They acquire the knowledge of the holy and crave divine intelligence. They seek solutions for life. My word dwells richly in their hearts and they dwell in the spirit of worship. Depression dissolves at their words and grief runs and hides in the dry places. The wise child will redesign the world with the wisdom that ushers from their mouth. Their words cannot be resisted, rejected or made powerless. The wise child is an answer waiting to happen.

TODAY I PRAY...

Psalm 31:20 over my children. They will feel hidden in the secret place of God's presence. They will be safe from all conspiring people that try to work against them. They will be immune to the nasty, mean and cruel words that are spoken to them because they are hidden in the Presence of the Lord.

...IN THE NAME OF JESUS.

THE HUNGRY HEART

God, you are my God; earnestly I seek you; my soul thirsts for you; my flesh faints for you, as in a dry and weary land where there is no water.
Psalm 63:1 (ESV)

Children gifted with a hungry heart save themselves from death. Hunger is the only way to extinguish all forms of worthless living. Holy hunger transforms the normal into the spectacular, the average into the amazing, and the obscure into the wonder working. Hunger is the key that unlocks heaven. The hungry will see me and be satisfied with my plan for their lives. The hungry always find the bread of life. They never starve for what truly matters. The hungry have no quit. They will try until they win. They will pursue until they obtain. They will chase until they catch heaven. The hungry pound at my door over and over again. They chase my will until it reveals itself. They are allergic to apathy, laziness and passiveness. The hungry child seeks my answers. They crave attainment. They long for divine similarity. They will search and cry and groan until the doors are open. They are the carriers of the fires of heaven. They are known as the torches of heaven. They spread holy desires. They throw fear to the wind. They do what I would never ask, but must be done. The hungry child knows that I am a God of desperation. Whenever someone comes to me in divine hunger and desperation, whatever they ask is granted. The holy things have been through the fires of testing. The hungry child, your child, will receive the word with eagerness and longing. They shall love what I love and hate what I hate. They shall seek where the narrow gates are and find them and love them. At the narrow gates, they will find the treasures for which they have longed. A child of hunger is already half way to their destiny.

TODAY I PRAY...

Isaiah 12:2 over my children that they shall draw water out of the wells of salvation and have great joy in doing it. They will never be thirsty because Jesus will satisfy their thirst. They will never be lost because they will have salvation in their minds, hearts, and spirits. Every day they will find the well of God and drink from it until they are fully satisfied with Jesus.

...IN THE NAME OF JESUS.

THE WINGS OF THE DOVE

In the six hundred and first year, in the first month, the first day of the month, the waters were dried from off the earth. And Noah removed the covering of the ark and looked, and behold, the face of the ground was dry. Genesis 8:13 (ESV)

I will carry your children on the wings of the dove. Their lives shall be a mirror of divine assistance. I will teach them how to ride on the currents of divine help. For my Spirit shall come upon them and they shall heal the sick, break the yokes and open prison doors. They will teach the secrets of the hidden manna. They shall pray with divine empowerment and have a lifetime of answered prayers. My spirit of wisdom shall rest upon them for the decisions they make. They shall have the spirit of understanding. They shall know the end of a thing before it happens. The spirit of my council shall be theirs. They will rest in the deep knowledge of my holy, healing ways. The spirit of might shall give them the ability to move enemy forces out of the situation and the spirit of knowledge will let them know what I know about what they do. The spirit of truth shall clothe them and council them in the night. They shall receive songs of deliverance in the night and escape self-imprisonment. The fear of me shall protect them from the unknown. I will guide them into paths of mercy and kindness. Their personality shall be a healing medicine. He will bring great conviction and repentance through your children. They shall be arrows of convicting truths. Many shall be saved. My spirit shall lead many of my sheep out of the wilderness into the Promised Land. I will give them a new heart and a new spirit. They shall cling to me like a grapevine. They shall continually bring forth the powers of the dove. They shall cherish the wings of the dove.

TODAY I PRAY...

Revelation 4:11 over my children. They will know they are created for God's pleasure and they are made to be His temple of worship. Today, the spirit of worship will be on my children and they will praise and adore God all day long and it will become their lifestyle.

...IN THE NAME OF JESUS.

HONESTY'S ARMS

The integrity of the upright guides them, but the crookedness of the treacherous destroys them. Proverbs 11:3 (ESV)

Honesty's arms are the hiding place of the transparent. I live where light rules. As a healing parent, honesty is your key to truth's riches. Your children will believe what they see you living. They will repeat what they hear you say. Honesty is heaven's soap; it washes the conscience from guilt and shame. Dishonesty opens the cages of your soul's enemies. A child trained in honesty will never lack the presence of love, the authority of heaven or the favor of truth. The healing parent hides their children in honesty. They sift their souls into the armor of transparency. The devil feeds on lies. He controls the liar and deceiver. You are your child's conscience until, like a vine, they grow one. Honesty tears down the bricks of lying thoughts. Honesty paints the face of God on the mind of a child. It shields them from the darkness that walks in the shadows of the night. Honesty is penicillin to the confusions of life. You are a healing light to your children. They deserve to be covered in the powers of honesty. Honesty keeps the divine lights on. When honesty begins, life begins. The light in your eyes will imprint itself on your child's soul. It will never forsake them. It will build bridges from blessing to blessing, from joy to joy and from victory to victory. Honesty in you becomes a crusade in your children. Clap for honesty and they will never betray themselves. Reward them for their truth telling and they will live to proclaim the truth. An honest parent creates an incorruptible child!

TODAY I PRAY...

Revelation 3:8 over my children. They will have the spirit of favor that opens doors for them. They will be led to open doors that no man can shut on them. When God opens a door, it remains open and when He closes a door, it remains closed. I bless them today with an open-door life.

...IN THE NAME OF JESUS.

FEASTS OF LAUGHTER

Then our mouth was filled with laughter, and our tongue with shouts of joy; then they said among the nations, "The Lord has done great things for them." Psalm 126:2 (ESV)

The healing parent is a sanctuary of joy. They heal with their infectious joy. They mend with laughter. They remove fear from their children's souls. Laughter is soul armor. Laughter is how you tell me that you believe everything is going to be alright. Your joy will send heaven's melodies into your children's hearts. A laughing child is a healthy child. A child that can laugh habitually is a magnet of heaven. The world is a broken and sad place. Man has lost his way. He is a ship at sea with no rudder. You can prevent your children from wandering by creating a home full of laughter and joy. If you don't have it, ask me to give it to you. I promise I will. You are a healer. You are a well of joy. You will not be dominated by grief, sadness or depression. Your children will be like the stars in the heavens, shining brightly with laughter. They will heal their world. Abide in me and dwell in my joy. Your children will go where you lead them. Reunite the fingerprints of their soul. Lightheartedness is medicine. Make your children joy addicts. A child that laughs with heaven's joy is not often sick. Divine, permanent laughter is the result of knowing how life ends. To play without burdens cracks open the pearls of life. A child who celebrates in the face of nay saying is: a David defeating Goliath, a hope defeating a fear, a faith reducing a mountain and a love rescuing the world. The hand of gloom and doom will never touch your joyful children; they will be the torches of victory!

TODAY I PRAY...

Over my children Luke 10:19. They shall tread upon the serpent. They shall tread upon the enemies of their soul. They will not be poisoned by any snake or defiled by any lies trying to come into their mind. Nothing shall by any means hurt them. They are holy unto You, Lord.

...IN THE NAME OF JESUS.

ERASING THE UGLY PAGES

"Remember not the former things, nor consider the things of old.
Behold, I am doing a new thing; now it springs forth, do you not perceive it? I will
make a way in the wilderness and rivers in the desert..." Isaiah 43:18-19 (ESV)

The ugly pages of life are erasable. The things that your children have seen, felt and known shall be erased. Their lives are claimed. I claim your children as my own. I will restore all of their years, even the years that the worms have stolen. I will restore life where the worms have touched. The locust, the canker worm, the caterpillar and the palmer worm each devour a different piece of life. One eats the roots and another eats the outside (or the identity). Another drills through to the heart and, finally, one eats the precious fruit. Your children shall be restored to wholeness. They shall eat in plenty at my table. They shall be satisfied with the loving-kindness of my house. They shall praise me for my great goodness and mercy. I will send times of refreshing from my presence and fruitful seasons. They will be lead on the path of beauty and salvation. The ugly pages shall be rewritten, redesigned and recolored. I shall be to them a restorer of life's meanings. I shall recalibrate the heartbeat of their soul. I will be their nourishment, filling them with the finest riches of heaven. They shall live above dismay, discouragement and despair. Their place of refuge shall be my presence. They shall plunder the enemy and recapture destinies for many that are lost in the wilderness of life. They shall unlock the treasure chests of heaven and pour out blessings upon their heads. I nullify every other harvest and loose them to read the new, revised pages of their lives.

TODAY I PRAY...

Psalm 36:6-8 over my children. They will see light in His light and will drink from the river of His pleasures. No elicit, illegal, or immoral pleasure will find honor in their hearts or captivation in their minds. I pray they will drink of the pleasure that comes from serving God, knowing God, and loving God all the days of their life.

...IN THE NAME OF JESUS.

THE IDENTITY JOURNEY

Therefore, if anyone is in Christ, he is a new creation. The old has passed away; behold, the new has come. 2 Corinthians 5:17 (ESV)

Every child must take their identity journey: who they are, where they are going and how to get there. These questions will be answered rightly by me and wrongly by others. The identity of a child is my passion. I am in constant movement to reveal to them the royalty in their existence, the pricelessness of their being, and the originality of their creation. I am engraving into their innermost being that uniqueness that will define them. I am at work chiseling away the unneeded stone around the masterpiece that is them. For in their identity, all their questions are answered. Every assignment is there waiting to be revealed. Every strength and every piece of divine direction is there, inside there divine identity. In their divine identity, every choice is pre-made. There every gift has been given, gifts of personality, light, power and empowerment. It is all there in their divine identity. They are wrapped in wisdom, throbbing with grace, burning with divine fire, running towards me, ever fixed and ready to obey and conquer. Their identity is their assurance, their inner confidence and their boldness to achieve what has never been done before. They are complete and fully formed in my mind. They are 100% functional in the divinities. They are a new creation, even before they are seen, discovered or explored. They are a wave of spectacular inventiveness and a descending surprise of grace. You children are royalty unfolding, a river of medicine running over the rocks and dams of life bringing Christ-likeness to the world.

TODAY I PRAY...

Isaiah 41:18 over my children. God will open the Heavens and send down a river of power, of love, of unstoppable mercies to my children. They will be full of the rivers of God that flow out of them.

...IN THE NAME OF JESUS.

THE SHOES OF THE CARPENTER

For to this you have been called, because Christ also suffered for you, leaving you an example, so that you might follow in his steps. 1 Peter 2:21 (ESV)

What would Jesus do? This is the life motto of a healing parent. They teach their children to ask this question in every good and difficult situation of life. They are a living lighthouse for their children. They reveal me to their children by inquiring what my Son would do, because he is in perfect oneness with me, the perfect expression of my divinity, and my image in action. He walks and the world is healed. He speaks and the true world is born within the seeking soul. One right question can save the world, create a true seeker and birth destinies. Divine questions existing in your child are their deliverance. To inquire of me is to save your future. To ask before you act is to prevent disasters. A child trained in divine inquiry will never wander from the path of life. To ask is to be led. Questions demand answers and the right answers perfect life. What would Jesus do? To ask this is to teach your child how to walk hand in hand with me. Wherever I am miracles happen, healings are released, power is manifested, and restoration is found. What would Jesus do? The healing parent creates a seeker; a child with divine questions will never be lost or walk alone. All the secrets are unlocked by these questions. A child with answers is a ever expanding universe of divine possibilities, a solution to a question, a cure in a searching world, and a medicine in an infirmary. Every child that has a library of questions receives answers. With each day, your children ask their way to me.

TODAY I PRAY...

John 7:37-38 that out of my children's spirit will flow rivers of living water. The river of revelation, the river of patience, the river of strength, the river of kindness, the river of mercy, the river of understanding, the river of the fear of God, and the river of clarity. Every day the living rivers of God will flow out of their spirit onto anyone they encounter.

...IN THE NAME OF JESUS.

THE SAVING GRACES

The greatest among you shall be your servant. Matthew 23:11 (ESV)

The healing parent flows with selfless love. He or she is addicted to serving under and in all contrary conditions. I love your selfless life, for in it, healing flows to your priceless children. Tyrants are over indulged children who do not ever learn the powers of selflessness. My Son's power flows from his selfless, self-sacrificing life. Never give into your desires. They will spread like a vine of disease. They will stop your rivers and wells from flowing. Selflessness is grace in action. Selflessness is the nature of healing transferred to your children. What you nurture you become. Selfishness is a dog with no confidence in their next meal, no trust in their masters goodness and generosity. Teach your children the art of open hearted, open handed living. A selfless child will become a storehouse of divine sufficiency. Give your children the gift of self-surrender. Teach them to say no to their personal selfishness and you will give them the true wealth of heaven. Selfish people are despised and rejected. Selfless children are trophies of love and grace. A healing parent lives at the feet of love's selfless desires. They are the guardians of the true and genuine ways of heaven. You are the selfless healer who prefers serving and sacrificing with no fear of losing out on the joys of life. Free your children forever from the chains of self-serving, self-gratifying, and tormenting wants and desires. Let them fly into the house of divine satisfaction.

TODAY I PRAY...

Isaiah 53:5 over my children. Jesus was wounded for their transgressions. He was bruised for their iniquities. He was chastised for their peace. By His stripes, they are healed. I pray my children will have these four anointings upon them: They will be able to dismantle iniquities, infuse peace, be conduits of healing, and be able to stop torments in the minds of men and women whom they come in contact with.

...IN THE NAME OF JESUS.

INTO THE ABUNDANCE

The thief comes only to steal and kill and destroy. I came that they may have life and have it abundantly. John 10:10 (ESV)

I know the struggles of your life and the tests and trials of your family. Fear not, the abundant life shall belong to your children. I will trust them into the abundance and drive out all thieves: the Amalakite, the Amorite, the Jebusite, the Perisite, the Hittite, the Hivite and the Caananite. I will drive out all of these tribes from your children's destiny. Into the abundance, I will send them. The abundance is the place of unlimited resources, spiritual completion, and where the table is full of all necessary provisions. Lack, poverty and half full are extinguished. I am abundance and your children shall never lack. I will guide them continually, satisfy their desire in scorched places and make their bones fat. They will be like a watered garden whose water never fails. Their delight shall rest in my word. They shall be addicted to my word and whatever they touch shall prosper. I will supply all their needs. I will open the door of abundant fellowship; I will thrust them into the abundance. They shall be rich in good works. They shall be outrageously generous and turn the tide of poverty for many. For I have formed their inward parts; I have knitted them together. They are full of beauty and abundant life. I will do more than is expected, more than is believed for and more than life can bring. Into the abundance, they will come.

TODAY I PRAY...

Isaiah 40:29-31 over my children. They will mount up on wings like eagles. They will ascend and climb and reach the heights of God's calling in their life. They will not be tired, weary, faint, give up or quit. They will have a spirit of unstoppable faith all the days of their life.

...IN THE NAME OF JESUS.

DESTINY'S CHILD

For I know the plans I have for you," declares the Lord, "plans to prosper you and not to harm you, plans to give you hope and a future. Jeremiah 29:11 (NIV)

A child of destiny is a preconceived life miracle. They do not possess the wasted life gene. They are world changers, blessed from the womb, ordained for greatness, settled into grace, marinated in faith, formed in Christ, and developed at Calvary's feet. They are heaven grown, driven by holiness, possessed with love, inspired by kindness and sculpted by goodness. They are the mirrors of pricelessness and the fruit of eternal planning. Destiny's children, your children, will alter ideas, change the conclusions of lost people, ratify the demonic loves of the land, and invent and discover philosophy cures. They will bring war to the entrenched beliefs of death and the ingrained values of self-destruction. They will be rooted in love and know the holy ways of the divine life. Love driven children reaping goodness, impart mercy, and embrace the divine tolerance of the kingdom of heaven. They will enact the movement of divine passion and cure the wounded, betrayed and soul crippled people. The child of destiny wakes up with destiny's heartbeat and they will not follow another. I am their destiny; I make them unshakable in conviction. I give them armor for their ideas and lead them in the everlasting way. I secure their future. I fortify them with enchanted, immovable beauty that flows out of their God touched personality. Destiny's children have free access to Eternity!

TODAY I PRAY...

Matthew 5:8 over my children. They that hunger and thirst after righteousness shall be satisfied. I pray the spirit of hunger over my children: hunger for God, His will and to satisfy their destiny. They will fulfill their calling in God and have a hunger to know all of His plans for their life. All day long they will hunger after God and be satisfied with the righteousness of His Kingdom.

...IN THE NAME OF JESUS.

CHILDREN OF THE CROSS

For the message of the cross is foolishness to those who are perishing, but to us who are being saved it is the power of God. 1 Corinthians 1:18 (NIV)

The cross bearing powers of trust release the wealth of heaven. The cross carrying child knows their purpose and lives with their carnal man nailed to the cross. All of heaven worships at the mention of the cross and resurrection. A child of the cross is a victorious, divine seeing child. They do not drink the privileges of selfishness. They do not feed on the bread of idleness nor do they give in to their unruly urges and impulses. I can trust a child trained in the art of self-crucifixion, nailing the old Adam to the cross daily. The old Adam gets no breath or life support, only nailed to the cross. If anyone would follow me, let him deny himself, pick up his cross and follow me. The word of the cross is the power of life. I gave my Son to be an example of how to live life, from daily death to daily death. Daily death is the way of grace. You have been crucified in my Son. You no longer live, but I live in you. Without carrying the cross, you are unworthy of the call. The cross child knows this. I am the author and perfecter of your children's faith. I teach them to despise the shame of worldly persecution and to embrace the honor of being shamed. I have canceled the record of wrongs, the life indictments, and erased the book of debts and all accusations against them. They are born out of freedom and love possessed children of the cross. They are set aside for my exploits.

TODAY I PRAY...

Isaiah 43:18-19 that my children will not be plagued with painful memories of the past. They shall know that a new thing is being done in them. They have new beginnings in God, and God will make a roadway in the wilderness for them, a river in the desert places of their life. They will always know where the rivers are. When they enter the desert, they will locate a river. When they hear the past, they will locate their healing.

...IN THE NAME OF JESUS.

THE WORD RULED CHILD

Jesus answered, "It is written: 'Man shall not live on bread alone, but on every word that comes from the mouth of God. Matthew 4:4 (NIV)

The word ruled child is the most influential child in Heaven and on Earth. My word is evaluating, incorruptible, and incomparable. My word is flawless, powerful, and life-altering. My word is healing, health and wealth. My word is milk, meat and bread. My word is rain, snow and seed. My word is a hammer of fire and a sword. My word is life and established forever. My word holds the universe together. I honor my word above my name. My word is a shield for the heart and mind. My word is a lamp and a light for your feet. My word is the standard for all living. I will place my word inside your children. I will engrave my beliefs in their heart. My word shall guide their decisions and sculpt their conscience. My word shall activate their faith and design their moral convictions. My word shall remain in their inner most being, caring and taking deep root in them. It shall keep them while they sleep and heal them from life's hurts, wounds and deceptions. They shall be like young oaks, standing tall and breathing in and out the breath of life. Every verse they memorize will become a manifestation of all things perfect. My word shall rule them and dominate their emotions. They shall live outside the reach of evil men. They shall have extraordinary gifts. Their intelligence shall be divinely outrageous. The word ruled child is the child of perfected harmonies.

TODAY I PRAY...

Lamentations 3:20-22 over my children. The steadfast love of the Lord never ceases over my children. His mercies never come to an end for them. Whenever they feel they have failed or made a mistake too big to cure, they will be reminded that if not for the compassion of God, they would've been destroyed. But it is the steadfast love of the Lord that never ceases, and His mercies never come to an end. They will know deep in their hearts that His mercies are new every morning.

...IN THE NAME OF JESUS.

THE RAIN DANCE

He will give the rain for your land in its season, the early rain and the later rain, that you may gather in your grain and your wine and your oil. Deuteronomy 11:14 (ESV)

I am the God of the rain. I send the rain to soften the soil of the heart and prepare the ground for my hundred fold seed. Rain refreshes the soul. It ends droughts and turns the wilderness into a garden. Rain is the presence of my being invested into the lives of those in famine. It is an answered prayer poured out. It is life realized. It is grace wrapped thinking and joy filled living. It is the absence of spiritual starvation. Your children are the rain. They are the latter rain that commands the seeds to come down. When the rains come, the fruit comes. All fruit is a divine encounter with me. Children of the rain bring breakthroughs. The rainy season is the divine season when all living seeds explode with growth. It is the season when the land and the trees of the field yield their increase. I will make your children divine storm clouds that are full of life and the wet rains of heaven. They will soften the hard-hearted and prepare the fields of Zion. They shall make life sprout and give seed to the sower and bread to the eater. They shall know the secrets of the rain dance. I will come to them, your children, like the showers that water the earth. They shall never experience permanent thirst or drought. They shall be known as drought breakers. They shall hear the sound of the abundance of rain. The clouds shall pour down showers of righteousness. Your children shall be continually rained on with fruitful seasons and I will satisfy their hearts and harvests.

TODAY I PRAY...

Matthew 14:24-26 over my children. Like Peter, they will say to Jesus, "Bid me come." They will have the power and faith to step out of the boat and walk on the waters of life. They will not be captivated or enslaved by fears or lying, intimidating thoughts. They will not be held back or be double-minded or unstable in any of their ways. They'll launch out, step out, and do God's will, walking on water all the days of their life.

...IN THE NAME OF JESUS.

THE SACRED FEET

When I saw him, I fell at his feet as though dead. But he laid his right hand on me, saying, "Fear not, I am the first and the last..." Revelation 1:17 (ESV)

There is a place of transformation where wholeness is obtained. There is a place where fear goes to die and champions are born. There is a place of illumination where the shadows flee. There is a place where trouble becomes mute and loneliness flees away. There is a place of divine encounters with heavenly creatures and where no dark, insidious thing can grow. There is a place where lies lose their validity and pain loses its power to punish. There is a place that must be sought out like hidden treasure. It must be chased even into eternity. There is a place where thousands go and find the answers to their needs. This place is a place of divine viewing, where all things come into perfect focus, balance is restored, the broken are mended, wild hearts are tamed and the rebel soul is cured. It is a place like no other on Earth or in Heaven. It is an eternal place where children find love, acceptance and completeness. A place where orphans are defined and the weary traveler finds his spring of living water. It is the place of the sacred feet of the lamb. Your children will be children who pursue home and places of rest. They will pursue the place of the sacred feet which calls out to them day and night. It calls out for them to come and let their burdens go. Come unto me and find peace for your souls.

TODAY I PRAY...

Luke 5:1-7 over my children. They will launch out into the deep mysteries of God. They will search out the secret things of God. Their nets will never be empty but always overflowing with fish to the point of breaking. They will have teams of boats that work with them, and all those boats will always be filled with provision and have more than enough.

...IN THE NAME OF JESUS.

NO BROKEN COMPASS

I will instruct you and teach you in the way you should go; I will counsel you with my loving eye on you. Psalm 32:8 (NIV)

Your children's compass shall not fail them. They shall find their true north. They shall not lose their way in the desert. No mirage shall lead them astray. No strange cove of lying sirens shall call to them out of the darkness. They shall not take a wrong turn. They shall always be able to find their way again. Their compass is unbreakable. It cannot lie and it will guide their feet to life and peace. Their compass is controlled by my hand. I occupy the past, present and future at the same time. I am in your past now, and I am healing it. I am in your present, arranging it. And I am in your future, preparing it. I am their inner compass. I will be their shepherd. My rod and my staff shall guide them in the everlasting way. I will guide them to springs of the water of life. No blindness shall attach itself to them and I will make them a light to those who sit in darkness. The spirit of truth shall govern them. Whatever they hear me speak, they will speak. Whatever they see me do, they will do and I will reveal to them what is to come. There are no pits that they will permanently fall into. I will remove the shadow of death from them. They shall see my road marks and guideposts. I will direct their minds to the highway of holiness, for they will lead the blind by a way they have not known. I will make darkness light before them and crooked places straight. These are the things I will do. I will not leave them undone.

TODAY I PRAY...

Psalm 20:2 over my children. The Lord will be their Helper today. They will sense that they are not alone. They are not fighting alone, learning alone, living alone, or dealing with life alone. The Holy Spirit is there for them today, and they will sense Him, be aware of Him, and love Him. They will have peace because the Lord is their Help in times of trouble. The Lord will be with them.

...IN THE NAME OF JESUS.

PERSUADED

"...being fully persuaded that God had power to do what he had promised."
Romans 4:21 (NIV)

Only those persuaded into full, unwavering faith can become invincible. The persuaded have been purged of all their doubts and questions. They live convinced and unyielding in the battles of life. The persuaded live in unconditional obedience. They know the answer before the question is asked. They say yes before the mission is revealed. They live on the waters of trust and faith. They waste no time pondering, analyzing or speculating about life. They have a resolved mind. They are a complete gospel and a finished portrait of Grace. The persuaded child does not waste years following the wrong mentors, teachers or guides. The persuaded child has no question marks in their perception, no alternate views in their perspective, and no unsolved mysteries in their conclusions. The persuaded do not fear their choices. Double-mindedness has been purged from their mental library. They are positively persuaded that I am able to guard and keep that which they have committed to me. They lean on, rely on and develop complete dependence on my Holy Spirit to guide them into all truths. They are eternally sure and positively convinced that I am their I AM. They do not stagger at my promises in unbelief, but are convinced that what I have promised, I am also able to perform.

TODAY I PRAY...

Over my children Romans 16:20, that they will know the God of peace has crushed Satan under His feet. They will not fear Satan or be afraid of his presence, voice, actions, or deeds. My children will see Satan as defeated under the feet of Jesus.

...IN THE NAME OF JESUS.

UNCONDITIONAL OBEDIENCE

If my people who are called by my name humble themselves, and pray and seek my face and turn from their wicked ways, then I will hear from heaven and will forgive their sin and heal their land. 2 Chronicles 7:14 (ESV)

Those who obey me, truly love me. I am raising up an army of obedient children, those who unconditionally obey my word. The obedient trust, believe and are supported by all the armies of heaven. To obey is divine. To obey is to move out of the way and allow me to move and create miracles. Those who master the art of obedience are trusted by me. I can trust someone without their own opinion. I can help someone who understands that I know what they don't. To obey is to understand the difference between the human and the divine. The child of unconditional obedience has already placed themselves in the hollow of my hand. Some obey from guilt, others from fear. Yet others obey for profit. Still others obey to please or for fame. But there are those who obey from love, simple, pure, and undefiled love. Obedient children have received the fear of the consequences of disobedience. Obedience brings rewards, while disobedience brings pain. Obedience is the key that unlocks the storehouses of heaven. All blessings are linked to an act of obedience. The disobedient inherit wrath, judgment and death. Your children will be given the divine gift of always saying "yes" to me and "no" to the devil.

TODAY I PRAY...

Ephesians 6:9-19 over my children. They will stand firm in the Lord and know their battle is not against flesh and blood but principalities and powers and rulers of darkness. Today, my children will put on their armor and walk in full protection. They will have the helmet of salvation for their mind, the breastplate of righteousness for their heart, the girdle of truth for their integrity, the shoes of the Gospel of Peace for their ministry, a sword of the Spirit for their wisdom, and a shield of faith for their protection. They will pray and know God all the days of their life.

...IN THE NAME OF JESUS.

THE OVERFLOW LIFE

You prepare a table before me in the presence of my enemies; you anoint my head with oil; my cup overflows. Psalm 23:5 (ESV)

I will send the overflow to attach itself to you and your children. I will send a great abundance of character, virtue, love and faith. They shall not be trampled or cursed under the feet of worldliness or experimental desires. They shall be steadfast, abounding in the essence of heaven. Their creed shall be courage, bravery in any circumstance, faith and loyalty at any cost, even their lives. Their greatest attributes will be grace, truth, and love and kindness for all. They shall overflow with goodness and mercy. They shall have the gift of unlimited spiritual resources. Their lives shall be blessed going out and coming in. Triumph shall mark them and advancement shall define them. I will make them increase in the land I have promised them. Excellence shall be their habitual behavior. They shall supply what is lacking to the saints and be famous for their unbridled generosity. They shall be unconstrained in their powers of discernment. Their ability to judge well shall protect them from the disguises of evil. All their days shall be spent in godly pursuits and adventures. Their cries of thanksgiving shall be heard throughout the land.

TODAY I PRAY...

Isaiah 65:24 over my children. Before they utter a prayer, they will know God has already heard that prayer. They will not doubt that their Heavenly Father hears their voice and answers even the prayers hidden in their mind and heart.

...IN THE NAME OF JESUS.

I AM WATCHING OVER THEM

Are not two sparrows sold for a penny? And not one of them will fall to the ground apart from your Father. Matthew 10:29 (ESV)

Through every trial of faith your children go through I will be there to persuade them. They shall have tests, trials and burdens, but I will uphold them with my hand. I will lead them with my power. I am watching over them. I will chase those that stray and convert those that doubt. I will save those that are lost and invade those that are preoccupied with life. Every one of your children is under my watchful eye. Keep praying; your prayers open the windows of heaven. Your children shall live with me, stand before my throne and serve me day and night. They will shout my victories and praise me for their redeemed lives. My sanctuary shall be their harbor and home. I will spread my tabernacle over them and fill them with my glory. Awe shall be their constant companion, worship their sword and obedience their armor. They shall be always with me. I am watching over them. I am protecting them from the evil influences. Their capacity to have an effect on those seeing truth shall be irresistible. They shall shape beliefs and ensure favorable treatment for the unwanted of the world. Their wealth shall never rust or decay, for it is the wealth of eternity. I am watching over them.

TODAY I PRAY...

Romans 12:1-2 over my children. They will present their bodies as a living sacrifice unto God. They will not sin with any portion of their body but walk in the holiness of God. They will not be conformed to this world but be transformed by the renewing of their mind. My children will prove what is the good, the acceptable, and the perfect will of God for their lives.

...IN THE NAME OF JESUS.

THE CHAMPIONS OF HEAVEN

For everyone who has been born of God overcomes the world. And this is the victory that has overcome the world—our faith. 1 John 5:4 (ESV)

I am the God of the orphan and the widow. I love and bless those who help and rescue them. I will not leave your children as orphans, comfort-less, desolate, barren, forlorn or helpless. I will always be their loving father as they dedicate their lives to the poor, the orphan and the widow. Their sword shall shine in the light of my Son's approval. Remember and write this truth on the tablets of your children's hearts, that pure religion is to rescue and visit the orphan and widow. Pure love is giving love. It is pure and unblemished in my sight. The aim of their life will be to love with pure motives and keep themselves unspotted and uncontaminated from the world. In me the fatherless find hope and mercy. I will be the champion of the widow and will save and preserve them. Your children shall become the champions of the widow and orphan. They shall sound the trumpet of their needs and cry out in the streets of their hope and deliverance. Thousands shall be rescued through the efforts of your children. They shall end oppression, injustice, cruelty and exploitation. They shall open doors of escape through education, spiritual regeneration and the healing touch of love. They are the champions of heaven.

TODAY I PRAY...

Matthew 11:28-31 over my children. They will come to Jesus when they are weary and tired. They will know that His burden is light, and His yoke is easy. Because He is meek and mild and full of love and mercy, He will carry all their burdens and weight. They will be at peace, not having to carry things they cannot control, and not worrying about things they cannot change.

...IN THE NAME OF JESUS.

THE PATH OF LIFE

The way of life winds upward for the wise, That he may turn away from [a]hell below.
Proverbs 15:24 (NKJV)

The path of life is clear and narrow. There is not an abundance of choices on the narrow path. Everything is revealed in prayer. The path of life is the tree of life. I will cut a road through the jungles of life and you and yours shall walk safely through the snakes and wolves of the night. I will make your road smooth and plain. You will experience ditch-less living. I will give you happy feet, straight motives, clear thinking and sober calculating. I will make the sore and halting limbs cured. Your children are my handiwork and my divine workmanship created in my Son. They shall live the good life. They shall know my riches and how my judgments are unfathomable and unsearchable. They shall know how my ways are untraceable, mysterious and indiscoverable. Yet, I will shine the light on the gloomy paths of life. They shall blot out deception, recklessness, unscrupulousness and wickedness. They shall be drenched in my saving purpose. They shall be like a trumpet in the desert declaring, "Here is the way, walk in it." The path of life is the way of life. They shall make new paths and erase the well-trodden paths of death. They shall open the old paths of truth and unblock the path of life. They shall be the repairers of the broken highways of holiness that lead to the paths of life.

TODAY I PRAY...

Over my children, Genesis 22:8. They will know God will provide a Lamb for the sacrifices of their life. They will know that no matter what situation they ever face, God is their Source and Provider. Because of Jesus, the Lamb of God, they will have access to all the storehouses of His Kingdom. My children will know that they will never be poor, but rich with the wealth of true riches.

...IN THE NAME OF JESUS.

THE TABLE OF HEAVEN

You prepare a table before me in the presence of my enemies;
you anoint my head with oil; my cup overflows. Psalm 23:5 (ESV)

I will prepare a banquet hall for your children. It will be a place of celebration and exaltation and a place of divine feasts. The twelve loaves of the conquered will be there to commemorate their life of total surrender, the surrender of their mind, will and emotions. The surrender of their dreams, desires and false hopes will be celebrated. The loaf will show the surrender of their heart, conscience, intuition. They have surrendered revenge, pain and false intimacy. These loaves of bread shall ever be before me as a sign of worship. I will be there chef and prepare for you all a meal of divinities. I have taken the bread of my will and have blessed it, broken it and given it to your children. They will not be deceived by falsely blessed bread. They shall have the eyes of an eagle and see what is hidden from others. Their table shall be my table. Their food shall be my food. Inner wealth shall flow from them to a starving, famished world. There shall be no dogs at their table. Every year they shall have leftovers that will feed the famine cursed people, for your children are called to be famine breakers.

TODAY I PRAY...

Psalm 45:7 over my children. The Lord will give them the oil of gladness. He will pour grace upon their words and put salt on their language. When they speak, they will speak with great insight and revelation, even as Jesus did. People who hear them speak will be addicted and attracted to the words of everlasting life.

...IN THE NAME OF JESUS.

Help
RESCUE GOD'S
Children

According to Psalm 68:5, God is the Father of all orphans. As He guides and guards your family, join us in rescuing His children: the orphan and widow!

WHATMATTERSMM.ORG

MAKE A DONATION OR BECOME A MONTHLY PARTNER TODAY!

James 1:27
"Pure and genuine religion in the sight of God the Father means caring for orphans and widows in their distress and refusing to let the world corrupt you."
NLT

Thank you!

CPSIA information can be obtained
at www.ICGtesting.com
Printed in the USA
JSHW010346051020
8137JS00002B/2